TEACHING WITH VITALITY

TEACHING WITH VITALITY

Pathways to Health and Wellness
for Teachers and Schools

Peggy D. Bennett

OXFORD
UNIVERSITY PRESS

Oxford University Press is a department of the University of Oxford. It furthers
the University's objective of excellence in research, scholarship, and education
by publishing worldwide. Oxford is a registered trade mark of Oxford University
Press in the UK and certain other countries.

Published in the United States of America by Oxford University Press
198 Madison Avenue, New York, NY 10016, United States of America.

CIP data is on file at the Library of Congress
ISBN 978–0–19–067398–7

9 8 7 6 5 4 3 2 1

Printed by Sheridan Books, Inc., United States of America

CONTENTS

TEACHING WITH VITALITY

INTRODUCTION

At the age of five, dear reader, I walked into my first-grade classroom and fell in love with learning. I must have become seriously smitten, for not one year since that time have I *not* been in schools . . . and it's been more than sixty years!

My passions have been consistent: education, learning, teaching. Teachers, students, schools. Scholars, writers, thinkers. Seeking, studying, wondering. Writing, speaking, mentoring. I remain committed to helping my fellow learners as we navigate our way through our lives.

I did my first teaching as a fifth grader, when I showed a first grader how to tap-dance for the annual school play. Maybe that was when I got hooked on teaching. The majority of my career has been spent in university settings, guiding future teachers and working with children.

Through it all, I have been consistently drawn to the nuggets. Whether I'm reading a book, listening to a lecture, or studying great thinkers, the small gems of wisdom I've found have always made me shiver.

When I discovered a bit of simple wisdom, I felt it to my core. I would remember it. I would look for and ponder connections.

I would begin to see its scope and profundity, and I would try to tell everyone about the idea.

Those nuggets became my bedrock for trying to understand people. From my undergraduate days, I realized that I was privately more passionate about studying and understanding people than I was about studying and understanding music, which I had thought would be my career. Early on, I knew that my destiny was not on the performance stage: it was in teaching, writing, and mentoring.

In the 1990s, after a year of extreme conflict and adversity, I decided I wanted to learn about mediation. I wanted to understand how we experience conflict and what we can do to resolve it. I became certified in basic mediation, family mediation, and victim-offender mediation. For seventeen years, I have volunteered to mediate cases for Justice Court in Bozeman, Montana. Mediation continually teaches me about people: what hurts us, what threatens us, what reconciles us, what smooths our troubles.

The wisdom and humor of Martha Beck's monthly columns in *O, the Oprah Magazine* had fascinated me for years. So in 2006, after completing certification with Martha Beck, I was on fire with ideas and tools for helping us find our way out of slumps. As a Martha Beck–certified life coach, I most often share those ideas in group presentations, brief writings, and casual conversations.

This background may explain why I write the way I do in *Teaching with Vitality*. I have chosen to share with you the nuggets that have been most important to me. And, because I respect your busy schedules and multiple commitments, I aimed to keep each topic brief and to the point.

Take your time. Topics are intentionally compact so that you can give a quick read, put the book down, and think about the topic. Don't worry if you disagree. It may be enough to simply *know* about another option and compare it to your own habits of mind. Have conversations about the topics. Learn what others think and experience.

I am very comfortable with posing possibilities for you to try, in thought and action. But it is important that you should not substitute my opinion for your own . . . about *anything*. Simply consider and experiment if you choose.

As I mustered my thoughts and imagined you reading them, I wanted to convey that someone is cheering for you. And I wanted you to feel acknowledged for the exhausting frustrations and the exhilarating joys you experience in schools.

Reviving, aiming to be better, is perennial for teachers. It never stops. We never "arrive" and stay there. Maintaining healthy attitudes and behaviors, recalibrating our beliefs when warranted, and searching for what we want and need are vitally important in schools. I heartily support your quest.

Vitality, the liveliness within us, is precious and priceless. My wish is that when you need reviving, these topics will help you regain health and wellness. The beneficiaries could be everyone in your school, including you!

I | THE GIFT OF TEACHING

To bring up, to rear, to grow. To educate means that we take responsibility. We accept a fiduciary duty to do our best in raising all those in our care.

The labels "educator" and "teacher" signify positions of honor *and* responsibility. We lead others to learn and grow and flourish. We are constant seekers. We always search for better ways to help students, teachers, and schools thrive.

We work with the tall and the small who bring out the best in us, the "me" we like. We also work with those who bring out the worst in us, the "me" we wish were different. And we can handle it all.

Some enter the field of education with trepidation, worried about all the things that can go wrong. And things *will* go wrong. When we see ourselves behave in ways that disappoint us, it teaches us. We learn who we *do not* want to be, and clarify who we *do* want to be.

Maintaining *some* fear of failure is not necessarily a disadvantage. We can be afraid, yet just like a new mother with a newborn, we figure it out. We consult, reflect, experiment, and determine to be better . . . for the sake of our learners *and* ourselves.

Teaching is such a personal profession. We expose our skills every day. We see our limitations as well as our strengths. We demonstrate a patience that we may not have. We nurture, even when we feel detached. We know that our quest to learn more and do more is never-ending.

Our vitality, the life in our teaching, comes from our dedication to "growing" people, including ourselves. And the growing never stops. The challenges never stop. The changes never stop.

It is those ever-changing "seasons" of teaching that provide a pathway for us to become seasoned teachers.

- Teaching teaches us.
- Teaching elevates and inspires us.
- Teaching is a worthy and wonderful challenge.
- In teaching, as we rear, we are being reared.

Teaching is a gift.

2 | RETHINKING STUDENT SUCCESS

In today's education, occupational (economic) life is the focus of our attention. We want every child to succeed, and this has come to mean that every child should be prepared for college and the sort of work that requires a college education. What of all the children who will become bus and truck drivers, retail sales clerks, appliance repair people, construction workers, materials handlers, heavy equipment operators, railway engineers and conductors, house painters, plumbers, bakers, farm workers, beauticians, postal workers, cooks, waiters, hotel clerks, house and office cleaners, auto mechanics and sales people, dog and horse groomers, telephone/electric line workers, prison guards, hospital attendants, grounds keepers, maintenance workers, managers of laundromats and dry cleaning shops, installers of burglar alarms, carpet layers, window washers, steel workers, fishermen, sailors, caterers, cashiers, chimney sweeps, roofers, makers of china and glassware, decorators, musicians, florists, entertainers, moving men . . . and what would happen to our society if no one were willing to do this work? Do these people represent failures of schooling, or do we fail them when we lead them to believe that only economic success *is* success? (Noddings, 2003, pp. 453–56)

Teachers and parents can lose perspective when achievement is narrowly defined. What messages are we sending students when grades, test scores, and academic achievement are the criteria for "success" during their twelve plus years of schooling?

Many students who struggle in school thrive in their families, communities, and jobs *once they leave school*. For some, leaving school may be the first time they experience real success and a sense of personal, task-related satisfaction.

As we teach them and before they leave us, have we given these "non-achieving" students *hope* that they will have the tenacity to excel? *Confidence* that they will find their path? *Courage* to trust their ability to figure it out?

Many students struggle with undiagnosed anomalies that limit their capacity to learn school subjects. For those students whose minds cannot adjust to the "book learning" of schools, do we still communicate that we want the best for them? Do we let them know that they are worthy of our support and encouragement for their future? Do we let students know they are valued whether or not they meet our academic expectations?

Students are worthy whether or not they meet our hopes for them. A pediatrician once said, "Some of us make better forty-year-olds than fourteen-year-olds. And for some it's the reverse." Let's remember to nurture the forty-year-old as we teach the fourteen-year-old.

3 | A METAPHOR FOR TEACHING

Metaphors, or figures of speech, can offer images that help us visualize, understand, and remember the messages they represent. Metaphors are excellent tools for framing the meaning of events, communicating effectively beyond literal language, and paving the way for new insights on teaching and learning (Bennett, 1999, p. 50).

As an exercise, college students who intended to become educators were asked to create a metaphor to match their recent experiences teaching in a public school classroom. The metaphors these future teachers chose were revealing and insightful.

Students were asked, "What is the biggest change you see in yourself during these first four weeks of teaching?" With a slow Texas drawl, one young man captured the adventure that a beginning teacher can feel. Many of us can relate to this one!

Well, I compare it to skiing. This may sound silly, but that's what I keep thinking about. When you first get on skis, you can't control anything: you can't stop, you can't change directions, and you can hardly stand up. You just know you're going to get hurt and probably even die. And ever getting

9

better seems like an impossible dream. But then when you *do* get the skills to ski, you finally understand why everyone else is so excited about skiing! It felt that way when I first experienced a sense that I could control the class's behavior by the way I spoke to them and the way I helped them focus. I felt exhilarated! (Quoted in Bennett, 1999, pp. 50–51)

Exhilaration! We can find that type of high in teaching. When we toss away fears, when we polish our skills, and when we sow the seeds of doing our best, we vibrate with hope, eagerness, and confidence.

4 | ATTACHING TO THE OUTCOME

We do our best to prepare *all* students to pass a test. We are diligent about demonstrating everything necessary to receive a good evaluation. We are consistently cheerful and friendly to a difficult colleague. We accommodate the wishes of a doting parent to calm worries about her child's behaviors. We spend many extra hours rehearsing, practicing, and readying our students for a performance. We behave kindly and compassionately toward a staff member with the hope of smoothing a recent conflict.

Good intentions do not guarantee good results. We need to have good intentions anyway. So many problems in our lives and relationships can be solved, or at least alleviated, if we intend to do good, *no matter what the outcome.*

One reason that good intentions are so important is that we are setting a path for ourselves: we are purposefully and thoughtfully aiming to make something better by our words and actions. But, of course, we have no (or little) control over the outcome. No guarantees. We may be disappointed that the outcome is not what we wanted, but that is *always* a risk. And let's not allow the outcome to diminish the constructive nature of our intent.

When we attach to the outcome, we rely too heavily on expecting a desired result.

- If I am kind to her, she'll be kind to me.
- If I work hard to achieve this, I will be rewarded.
- If I try hard enough, I'll see the results I want.
- If I remove myself from the group, others will coax me back.
- If I sulk, others will know they have hurt me.
- If I share some gossip with a co-worker, we'll become closer friends.
- If I bring treats and gifts, others will see how clever and generous I am.

Imagine how our disposition would change if we crafted good intent with no attachment to the outcome.

- We would lessen our desire for acknowledgment of our efforts.
- We would lessen our disappointment when someone did not meet our expectations.
- We would lessen our dependency on others' confirmation of our good work.

In many ways, when we detach from the outcome that we initially expect and want, we free ourselves to be flexible, observational, and liberated from our own narrow thinking.

5 | BEHAVING RESPECTFULLY

"Respect your elders." "Show some respect." "He's my supervisor, I must respect him."

Respect is a *feeling* of esteem and admiration. Yet it is also a *behavior*, showing consideration and goodwill. These two manifestations of respect are important distinctions as we navigate relationships with others and choose our behaviors toward them. What we sometimes forget is that respect can simply be *behaved*. We can "behave our way into it."

We need not respect someone in order to behave respectfully toward them. And it is the "behaving respectfully toward" that maintains the health of schools and school relationships. At times when we do not feel esteem toward another, we can "behave our way into" what is necessary and best.

It is possible that respect more frequently involves behavior than attitude. For example, we may not have reason to *feel* respect toward everyone we encounter. How do we know strangers are worthy of our respect? Even for those who may not be worthy, we can *behave* respectfully toward them anyway. See the difference?

How do we make a habit of behaving respectfully? We behave *as if* we respect a person. We behave *as if* the person respects us. We behave in a manner that the situation calls for. And we make choices to be considerate, to show the best of ourselves, even though the other may not have earned or deserved our respect.

You may think adopting this calculated responsiveness aims to serve the other person. But it really serves us both. When we reserve judgment long enough to shift to *behaving respectfully*, we are the benefactors as much as the recipients are. We reframe negative assumptions. We give the benefit of the doubt. We suspend judgment. Each of these intentions serves our own mental, physical, and social health.

Imagine the possibilities for schools if teachers, parents, administrators, and students learn that behaving respectfully is something we can *all* do. Imagine a habit of mind in which behaving respectfully is an automatic balm for our spirits: it bolsters us, it gives us confidence, and it revitalizes our power to be generous and kind.

> By cultivating respect for others, we develop a kind of "relaxed diplomacy" that becomes part of our work style. Because we are considerate, we no longer need to apologize for being tough or straightforward; we no longer need to always make the safe decision or imagine the worst about work place difficulties. We develop the confidence to sense when to be tactful and restrained and when to be forthcoming and direct. (Carroll, 2006, p. 47)

6 | TEN-MINUTE MAKEOVER

Each of these seven suggestions can make over your presentation skills, give your teaching a lift, and better engage your students. As you become more aware of these lifts, watch and listen for good examples in others.

1. *Posture.* With feet about shoulder width apart, gently and slowly bend forward as far as you can, rolling your spine downward as you go. Keep your body loose and flexible. Roll up slowly with the image that you are stacking your vertebrae one at a time. Continue lifting through your spine to the top of your head. This posture of *tall* (a different image from *straight*) is very powerful. When you are tall and relaxed, you appear confident, courageous, strong. Summon this posture when you want to present the best of yourself.

2. *Eye expression.* Intentionally soften the area around your eyes. Feel the relaxed openness of your eyes, as if you are breathing in softness. Then, intentionally harden your eyes to see the contrast. Watch yourself in the mirror to spot the differences. Teaching calls for both expressions.

3. *Eye lingering.* With soft eyes that welcome listeners as you teach or talk, allow your gaze to linger momentarily when you pose a question or make a statement. Eye lingering avoids a darting look that can project worry or lack of confidence. And eye lingering can offer nonverbal support to the person answering your question or listening to your voice.

4. *Gestures.* Most of us struggle with how to gesture as we speak. Especially when we teach, our gesturing can be meaningful, helping to convey confidence and caring about our topic. Notice others who demonstrate good gesturing. Try their techniques. Aim to use fluid movements rather than jerky ones. Show open hands with palms up. Remove hands from pockets. Sometimes holding a book or paper with one hand makes it comfortable to gesture with the other.

5. *Voice projection.* Speak to those in the back of the room. Learn to project without shouting. Be vocally expressive as you amplify your normal speaking voice. When listeners struggle to hear, their ability and incentive to learn are greatly diminished.

6. *Vocal expression.* Our voice is our most valuable asset for teaching. Variety in pitch, pace, and volume is important to helping students sustain listening. Vary the *pitch* of your voice, sometimes inflecting upward, sometimes downward. Vary the *pace* of your voice, slowing your pace when you make an especially important point. Vary the *volume* by projecting a louder or quieter voice when you want to emphasize a point. These practices provide vocal expression that helps others listen and learn.

7. *Proximity.* As a simple way to elicit attention, vary your location in the room and your proximity to individuals as you teach.

7 | PRAISE IN THE CLASSROOM

If every time you walked into my classroom I handed you a dollar for no apparent reason, you might be initially surprised and happy. You might be curious about what you did to deserve the dollar. Then, as I gave you a dollar each day for the next two weeks, perhaps you would just shrug and say, "Well, she must think I did something to deserve this, and I won't argue."

As the daily dollar gift continues, you find yourself beginning to count on that dollar for a snack after school or savings toward a bicycle. You don't ask why I'm giving you this gift, and I don't tell. Then one day I stop.

When we are accustomed to receiving a reward, even if we are not sure we earned it, we can be startled and resentful when it stops. Somehow in our minds, the sudden absence of the expected reward gets interpreted as *punishment* (Bennett, 1988; Kohn, 1992).

We have a conundrum when a motivator (praise and rewards) demotivates. Too easily, the indiscriminate reward of praise creates mini-addictions in our students.

The intent here is not to ban praise and rewards from classrooms, but to use them with judicious, vigilant knowledge of their risks. Three aspects of praise help illuminate some of its risks.

1. *Gradations of compliments.* Students notice the varying levels of empty praise: "Very good," "Excellent," "Good attempt," "Okay." And they notice who consistently gets what praise. Substitute feedback that feeds: offer neutral, observational, and encouraging comments.

2. *Oppositional behaviors.* When we gush praise, thinking we are making students "feel good" and building self-esteem, we can often embarrass them instead. Teasing by classmates can prompt students to make errors to avoid a teacher's overt praise. Offer mostly observational comments, praise in private, and avoid overstated and overenthusiastic responses to students' efforts.

3. *Competition.* Many of us were taught to say things such as "I like the way Angie is sitting" to garner student compliance, especially for younger students. And for many of us, it worked! Are we, however, socializing students to be compliant rather than cooperative? When we say "I *like* the way Avery is . . . ," young children (especially) can hear, "I like Avery." An alternative to this practice is simply to omit "I like" and instead comment on what you see: "Avery is quiet and ready to listen." "Noah has his pencil ready." "Shelley found her spot and is ready to learn."

Handing out praise in learning settings has been compared to distributing candy: it tastes good and may momentarily satisfy, but it can also create an addiction to something that has little or no nutritional value.

8 | REAL MOMENTS

Can you remember a time when you were totally absorbed in the moment? When "the rest of the world" ceased to exist? When returning to your surroundings felt a bit jolting? If so, you may have experienced a "real moment."

Our "real moments" as teachers often happen when a student has an "aha!" experience. Or when we finally figure out how to present a confusing concept, and it works just the way we hoped. Or when there is such a meeting of the minds with fellow teachers that it feels like a wave of perfection has just rolled over us. And when they do occur, real moments can revitalize and invigorate us.

The trick to relishing these real moments is to *notice* them. Then we can acknowledge and savor them as bits of bliss.

According to Barbara De Angelis, "Real moments occur only when you are consciously and completely experiencing where you are, what you are doing, and how you are feeling . . . *you are paying attention*" (1995, p. 25). Paying attention is not necessarily as easy as it may seem. Having racing minds and darting attentions, we get in the habit of *not* paying attention. So may our students.

What can we do to *stop, drop,* and *be*? Simply *stop* thinking. Notice your surroundings. Listen and watch as others speak. *Drop* your hurry and worry long enough to breathe, feel, and notice what surrounds you. *Be* present to soak up all that your senses allow.

> You allow real moments to happen when you totally surrender into whatever you are experiencing, and let go of trying to be in control. (De Angelis, 1994, p. 26)

9 | I IS JUST I

"That's disgusting!" "His voice is so obnoxious!" "She is totally ineffective."

Each of these opinions has something in common: the statements are absolute, the opinions are delivered as universal truths. When we speak like this, we announce our feelings and beliefs as if there could be no reasonable disagreement. We skew the very real probability of multiple opinions, and we convince ourselves of our "rightness."

Are we all prone to treating opinion, especially ours, as fact? Maybe. What would change for us if we habitually acknowledge that our opinion simply represents "I?" The quotes above do little to elicit communication or invite conversation. "I" in those statements is just "I." But the "I" seems to imply, "I don't like it, and you shouldn't either!" Are we interested in the response of the listener? Do we ask?

When we accept that "I is just I," we humble ourselves to acknowledge we are sharing a perspective, not a decree. Then our language changes. Our perspectives change. We open ourselves to alternative ways of seeing and appreciating co-workers and students.

- "She is hopeless" becomes "She seems to struggle with these assignments."
- "He is a bully" becomes "He has some social issues going on."
- "She is a loser" becomes "She is struggling, and I hope she moves past this phase."

Those of us willing to acknowledge that "I is just I" temper our pronouncements about others. That softening of self can be felt inside our skin. We feel it in our eyes. We feel it in our breathing. We feel it in our spirit. And when we feel that softening, our vitality returns.

10 | ACCEPTING CHANGE

Transitions can be both exciting and frightening. A change may be our choice, yet we can still experience both optimism and anxiety, eagerness and resistance. We can fret about the results. We can become impatient. We can extinguish any pleasantness *during* the change by our worries *about* it.

Sometimes a metaphor can help soothe the throng of emotions that come with change. The image can give us ways to interpret, understand, and reframe. In this case, the metaphor that mirrors the angst of change is the way a snake sheds its skin and then gains renewal.

For snakes, shedding skin is a necessity: they *must* shed in order to grow. Snakeskin does not expand like our skin, so it becomes constrictive as the snake matures. Shedding also serves the snake by ridding it of troublesome parasites.

There is no good way to hurry the process of shedding. The snakeskin comes off in one piece during a very slow, tedious process that may include going for a swim or rubbing against a log to complete the sloughing. The main action during this tedious change is simply *waiting*.

Shedding can also be a somewhat dangerous time. As snakes shed their skin, their vision becomes increasingly cloudy. They begin to exhibit irritable, nervous behavior. They are more prone to strike out and be less "themselves."

The parallels seem obvious. Comparing nature's way of adapting to shedding skin and accepting change may offer us some optimistic perspectives.

A major frustration in schools is the constancy of change. Mandated curricular and procedural changes can be confusing, upsetting, and exhausting. There is often a period of time during a change when *everything* seems overwhelming. We resist, we complain, we consider early retirement.

Some of us love change; some of us hate it. Resisting and griping tend to offer no power, and they just make us more miserable, more tense, and less secure.

The image of skin shedding can help us adjust and accept. Change is a process that we cannot necessarily hurry or reject. While it is occurring, we may not see too well, we may exhibit irritability, and we may forget that "better" is on its way. During the process of change, we can simply wait. We can notice. We can let it be.

11 | ASSERTIVENESS AS NECESSITY

Pre-service and early career educators often struggle with delivering a command. Stern expressions feel mean. Vocal volume feels mean. Directives feel mean.

Yet assertiveness is necessary in schools and in life. And often the differences between assertiveness and aggression, cajoling and ordering, firmness and harshness need to be learned.

Using "Sit down" as a practice directive can allow experimentation with changes in posture, volume, tone, and facial expressions that accompany the Five Levels of Assertiveness (Chapters 12–16). When we know and can demonstrate appropriate levels of insistence, we can send the messages we want and need to send, both in schools and elsewhere. Five guiding thoughts can contribute to being as assertive as necessary:

1. *Support meaningful words with emotional confidence.* Words may sound automated and disingenuous if they are detached from meaning. Speaking as if reading a script is ineffective and takes a toll on our sense of authenticity. Assertiveness levels 1 and 5 have us emoting fear and anger, respectively. Yet the statements of levels 2, 3, and 4 have us integrating

emotion, intention, and wise words to evoke goodwill and healthy interactions.

2. *Plan for how you want to feel afterward*. When we imagine how we want to feel as a result of our encounter, we let those images guide our demeanor. Compassion and empathy can be a constant, heartfelt state of mind, but they need not be delivered with weakness. If we know we want to feel strong and empathic *after* an encounter, that awareness can manifest itself *during* the encounter.

3. *Monitor intent*. We can monitor our own words and feelings by asking, "What is my intent here?" If our intent is revenge, shaming (level 5), or disingenuous agreement (level 1), take time to reconsider and reword.

4. *Practice*. Initially it can be difficult to perfect the wording we want to use in tense or threatening situations. But like any other habit of mind, desirable words, feelings, and behaviors come more easily with practice.

5. *Stay open*. Effective assertiveness can be exhilarating. The strong and healthy middle levels of assertiveness (2, 3, and 4) are neither pandering nor punishing. They give us opportunities to behave without the inherent oppressiveness of levels 1 and 5. We state what is needed in a way that offers direction and a solution. We are as assertive as necessary.

12 | ASSERTIVENESS LEVEL 1

We are almost completely non-assertive when we operate in level 1. We say yes when we want to say no. We compliment someone simply because she expected it. We acted as if his joke was funny, even though we wanted to tell him how crude it was.

Of the Five Levels of Assertiveness, level 1 behaviors are the most deceptive. Functioning at this level hides us. We sacrifice our own peace in order to keep peace with others. We apologize for actions that warrant no apology. We agree publicly and fume privately. We can become so accustomed to repressing our own opinions that it may take some effort to regain our voice.

Subjugation and sublimation can become the unhealthy habits of level 1. Inauthentic and incongruous messages and behaviors can result.

- "Oh sure, I'm happy to do that for you" (resenting the request, but pretending otherwise).
- "I'm so very sorry that I didn't submit the report on time" (using untrue or inauthentic messages to save face).

- "You are so artistic. Your room is beautiful, and mine is so plain" (complimenting to invite a reciprocal compliment).
- "If you'll sit down and get quiet, maybe we can end class a few minutes early" (using a weak, non-authoritative plea to bargain for behavioral compliance from students).

A problem of level 1 behavior is that we go overboard to hide our feelings. And we do so to make other people believe we are not bothered by what they have said or done. We become a chameleon to fit in, for others' comfort. Our facial expression is often smiling with soft eyes, and we may use a highly inflected voice. In level 1, we are approval-seekers, willing to sublimate our own sense of authority in order to maintain peace. We appear sweet, kind, and gentle, but under the surface lie repressive discord and disharmony.

To be sure, there are times when we knowingly choose to respond in level 1. And there are times when this level of response may be best for both parties involved. Yet if we feel diminished and devalued during or afterward based on our deferential attitude, this level of response deserves some critical reflection.

| 3 | ASSERTIVENESS LEVEL 2

In the level 2 state of assertiveness, we are tranquil, assertive, and powerful. Our voice is calm. Our face is neutral to soft. We are fair-minded and strong. Conflict is easily and efficiently resolved. Neither apologetic nor needlessly assertive, our frame of mind in this stage is to take care of the problem quickly and efficiently, so that there is no longer a problem. We neither shrink from nor plow our way through the situation.

In level 2, we become adept at stating and displaying an adequate degree of assertiveness. Our actions in this level can be so adept that we hardly know there could have been a problem. The confidence that builds in level 2 becomes our norm, and potential conflicts dissolve with balanced and confident responsiveness. Harsh retorts and meek acquiescence are mostly things of the past as we hone our internal and external responses to potential conflict.

In the balanced state of level 2, our voice is matter-of-fact, moderate volume, non-threatening, and non-threatened. After much practice, this level becomes more of an automatic reframing and re-visioning of what is happening and what to do about it. Decisions that undergird responses in level 2 may be totally internal, when there is no need for a verbal or external response.

Inwardly and outwardly, we feel in near perfect balance. The other's behavior did not pull us out of our best self. It did not lure us into making a response that was unnecessary.

- In response to a waiter bringing the wrong order: "You may have thought I said pasta, but I ordered salmon. What is the possibility that you could bring the salmon in the next ten minutes?"
- In response to a noisy student interrupting another: "Allison, it is not your turn. Watch and listen to Meghan."
- In response to a very angry colleague, you choose not to get involved, and you watch the venting with detached observation. Or you calmly leave the scene.

Notice that responses in level 2 can carry with them a recommendation or suggestion for what to do next. These exchanges are handled with neutral, soft eyes. Our tone of voice is light, calm, matter-of-fact, informative, and conversational.

In level 2, we feel shielded from escalating conflict, because we know how to respond. And we avoid feeling threatened by the people or the problem.

14 | ASSERTIVENESS LEVEL 3

When the situation calls for a more assertive response than level 2, our face becomes more neutral, more detached. Our eyes shift from soft to neutral or slightly hard (see Chapter 25, "Eye Expressions"). The pace of our speech slows, and the pitch of our voice becomes less inflected. Our intent is to be clear and assertive in a way that needs little explanation. Our statement is brief, because the more words we use, the less effective our stance can become.

Confidence in using level 3 provides us with a sliding scale for being as assertive as necessary. Whether our message is delivered in person, on the phone, or in writing, its meaning and intent are uncluttered and clearly stated. Sometimes we use level 3 when the assertive message of level 2 is not being received. A level 3 response is one that has us standing our ground in ways that levels 1 and 2 do not.

Our state of mind when we convey level 3 assertiveness is calm, strong, and mildly commanding. Our message is both clear and succinct.

Imagine an administrator saying to you, "I've heard some parent complaints about your discipline, and I'd like you to go easy on the kids for a while." Many of us would have an immediate "hackles raised" reaction.

In level 3, we may say with focused confidence and strength, "I'm always open to conversations about what and how I teach. How soon could we schedule an appointment so you can tell me what you're thinking, and we can discuss this?"

In and out of school, level 3 responses provide a way to be strong, not brash; clear, not sarcastic; forceful, not oppressive. Whether managing students, negotiating with authorities, solving problems with a forceful parent, or replying to an angry stranger, we can maintain peace and power through our words and attitudes.

15 | ASSERTIVENESS LEVEL 4

More assertive and insistent than level 3, level 4 intensifies our verbal and nonverbal posture without taking us into the territory of hostility. The same words may be used as in level 3, but the delivery of those words is more intense.

Facial expression is very focused, with mildly hard eyes. We speak with an almost flat inflection in the lower part of our vocal range. We pronounce words with a crispness (especially consonants) that is very direct.

As in level 3, giving directives is important in level 4, and they help focus our intentions and expectations. In level 4, we are very firm in delivering our message, without using aggressive behavior or demeaning language.

- To a student who calls another student a derogatory name: "That is unacceptable in this classroom!"
- To a colleague who makes an inappropriate comment or gesture: "That has no place in our school. If you want to know why, ask me about it. Otherwise, just know I am voicing my objection to that right now."

- To a telemarketer who gets pushy: "This is my home. You are intruding. Do *not* call me again!"
- To a child who retorts, "I don't want to and you can't make me!": "You don't want to do that, and I don't especially want to *make* you do that. But we will sit here until it is done. So you have some choices to make right now."

Assertiveness level 4 delivers a strong "cease and desist" message. It conveys that something must stop; something must change. In this level of assertiveness, a line is being drawn with a powerful message, but harsh words that accuse, goad, or inflame are not used.

In some ways, level 4 lets us be strong, intense, and absolute without being pulled into the magnetic field of others' wrath or derogatory behaviors. The purposeful demagnetizing that level 4 offers can make lasting, potent contributions to our emotional health.

16 | ASSERTIVENESS LEVEL 5

In the fifth level of assertiveness, words are harsh, denigrating, and disrespectful.

1. A student uses profanity in the classroom. We shout, "How dare you use that word in my class! Anyone who talks like that is low-class and stupid! You may be both, but you will not use that word in my class again!"
2. A friend tells us he/she won't be able to keep a commitment. We shout, "You always do this to me! I should have known that I couldn't count on you to follow through. I don't know why I even try to plan something fun for us. Just go ahead and cancel—I'll find someone else to go with me who is more fun than you, anyway!"

The intent in level 5 is to scold, insult, and brandish power. In this level of assertiveness, there is no assertiveness, just aggression. We are mean-spirited, extinguishing nearly any immediate opportunity for peaceful reconciliation. Our facial expression shows hard eyes and extreme tension. Our tone of voice is loud or louder than normal, with an edgy, dismissive tone.

Level 5 is all about emotion and using false power to shame, demean, and degrade someone. At this level of anger and sarcasm, we diminish others, whether or not they are present to hear us, whether or not we speak our words aloud. If we are *thinking* this level of vitriol, we are also likely *feeling* it. And such venom moves us further away from the calm, centered core to which many of us aspire.

We may think that we are powerful as we ream another in level 5. But the power is false. We poison *ourselves* with the nasty words and extreme tension, even as we think we are upbraiding someone else. If we pay attention, we can see and feel the power leaking out of us as we show the *worst* of ourselves.

Level 5 is at odds with healthy schools, healthy teachers, and healthy living. Our level 5 behaviors take a toll on those receiving them and, sometimes even more strongly, on those witnessing them.

Level 5 aggression can make us sick. And teachers overstep their ethical boundaries when they behave as if they have the right to demean or degrade others in schools.

17 | HONOR IN BEING HONEST

- "You want my honest opinion?"
- "I'm just being honest."
- "I'm going to be brutally honest with you."

For many of us, hearing these words causes us to brace for mean-spirited "feedback." And when we are the one "being honest," we may believe we have unfettered permission to hurt, harm, or embarrass . . . all under the guise of honesty.

Too often, the speaker uses "I'm just being honest" to excuse himself or herself from a kind or tempered commentary. Think of the categories toward which this kind of brutal honesty is aimed: appearance, skills, integrity, home life, family members, level of education, and so on.

What is honesty, anyway, and why do we use it to say and do harsh and hurtful things? Why do we give ourselves permission to be impolite and to degrade someone under the banner of "being honest"?

The etymology of the word "honesty" may surprise you. In previous centuries, the original meaning had the same root as the word "honor": good manners, elegance, decency. Imagine how our verbal interactions might change if our honesty became honorable action.

Imagine how our vitality in schools may change when we aspire to interact with decency and good manners, to be honest with students as well as staff. Imagine how we might explain and demonstrate honor and honesty throughout our students' time with us.

- Rather than speak with unconstrained freedom to hurt and hinder, we would display honesty with honorable actions and elegant intent.
- Rather than equate honesty with "truth" (whose truth?), we would use honesty as the opportunity to behave with decency and good manners.

When we adopt such noble attitudes and behaviors, we feel vibrant. Our energy changes. Our sense of being both peaceful and powerful is clear. We know we are on rich, solid ground.

> Behaving the way we choose, rather than the way that feels most natural, is foundational to our own leadership, maturity, and ability to help our students grow and develop . . . . Perhaps we are closer to being honest with ourselves and others when we act the way we know is best for the situation and act the way we want to be rather than acting according to habit and what feels natural. (Bennett & Bartholomew, 1997, p. 150)

18 | FACING FEAR

Do you know what you fear? Some folks know the answer right away. Others need to think about it for a while.

Fears have a wide range of characteristics. Some fears may serve, others may hamper. What do you do about your fears? How do they affect you?

Many of us had a general fear when we began teaching. We may not have been able to identify what or who we were afraid of, but we *were* afraid. For teachers, fears of embarrassing oneself, of showing others how ill-informed and unprepared we are, and of being unable to "handle" students' behaviors are common. The very real fear about safety in schools is, sad to say, a potent concern as well.

Some believe that systematically dismantling fear helps. Others recommend that copiously proving how silly fears are can relieve us of them. Some believe additional information helps dissolve fears or puts them into perspective.

Have you ever considered how it would feel to be *fearless*? Take a moment to feel totally fearless. Were you able to do it?

What would change if you were at school every day without fear? When our state of mind is not shackled by fear, imagine what we could accomplish.

Letting fear consume us, no matter how impending we feel the danger to be, can skew our reasoning and taint our perceptions. Some of us even fear the fear! When Barbara Brown Taylor stated, "We'd like life to be a train, and it's a sailboat," she captured the sentiment that we often fall victim to our own fears and anxieties.

We would *like* a straight, predictable path. But we most often *get* a path that changes when we least expect it, that takes us places we never intended to go. And sometimes those places we go bring us exactly what we need.

So, rather than run from our fears, we can face them. Rather than worry, we can be fearless, even if momentarily. Rather than fret, we can calm ourselves. We can take a moment to consider that, beyond our limited vision, all may be well.

Take three deep breaths. Face your fear. Stand tall. Be brave.

19 | VALUING YOUR VOICE

If you have ever contracted laryngitis, you know the value of your voice. You feel fine. You are not contagious. You have much to do. You cannot make a good argument for staying home. Yet teaching without a healthy voice can be hard, hard work.

Our voice is our most precious instrument. Do we care for it as if that is true? These five suggestions can help you maintain a healthy voice.

1. *Balance of breath and muscle.* When vocal sound production is balanced with muscle and breath, we are generally using our voice properly. When more muscle than breath is used, a forced sound causes undue stress on our vocal folds, often resulting in a raspy sound. Support your voice with breath energy to help maintain healthy vocal production.
2. *Hydration.* Talking for lengthy amounts of time causes us to lose moisture through our breath. Don't wait until you're thirsty to drink water. Stay hydrated throughout the day.
3. *Avoid touching your face.* Our hands are often the germiest parts of our bodies. To maintain a healthy voice, avoid touching your face, especially during cold and flu season.

4. *Vary your vocal expression*. Variety in pitch, pace, and volume is good for our voices and good for our listeners. Vary the *pitch* of your voice by shifting between higher and lower tones. Speed up and slow down the *pace* of your speaking. Speak at louder and quieter *volumes* to help students listen.

5. *Lift your voice*. Speaking at the lower part of your vocal range, especially if you are projecting loudly to a group, can cause vocal difficulties similar to a callus on your vocal folds. For the health of your voice, lift it to a medium high range (say "mm-hm" as an agreement and stay at the "hm" level) and speak using plenty of breath energy.

The louder we talk, the less students need or want to listen! Try speaking normally rather than "talking over" noisy students; they will learn to respond. In physical education, music ensembles, and other large classes, a habit of shout-speaking can develop and derail your vocal health.

We need our voices . . . to display empathy and sternness, to speak loudly without anger, to speak softly to elicit attention. Our voices play a significant role in our teaching. It makes sense to care for them like the fine, valuable instruments that they are.

A positive and compelling voice image [is] a voice that draws you into its spell. Such a voice presents the substance and character of the speaker, as well as the content of his ideas, in a positive light. This is why I say that your manner of expression—and by this I refer to how you use your voice—is the key to your identity. (Cooper, 1984, p. 5)

20 | THE TEACHER'S CREED

Like a weather vane, we are sometimes buffeted by winds of change in our schools. Some of us hardly react to the shifting ambiance on any given day; we carry our own weather with us. Others of us become saturated by the mood and environment that cloaks us. Those buffeted by stormy challenges or adrift in strong currents need a buoy, a life preserver.

One way to identify our own buoy in schools is to choose sayings, poems, favorite quotes, and self-affirmations that can remind us of our priorities. Another is to have a set of principles that ground us.

Adapted from the physician's Hippocratic oath, the Teacher's Creed may help us in times of rough seas. Imagine how these intentions could be touchstones for being our best in schools.

Teacher's Creed
1. *Non-maleficence*: Do no harm.
2. *Beneficence*: Do good.
3. *Justice*: Treat fairly.
4. *Autonomy*: Honor self-determination and the right to choose.

Do no harm. We commit ourselves to the intent to do no harm (emotionally, physically, spiritually, academically) for all constituents in our schools.

Do good. We act on the commitment to nurture and inspire learning for the benefit of all in our schools.

Treat fairly. "Fair" and "just" have many layers. Fair is not necessarily equal, and justice is likely debatable. Most important is our commitment to stay open to the evolving meanings and treatments that constitute fair and just for our students and co-workers.

Honor self-determination and the right to choose. We acknowledge that we may never know what is best for another, and the other may have the right to be wrong. Allowing another to determine what she/he wants and needs can be wrenching. Yet acknowledging the sovereign will of others propels growth, no matter our age.

21 | PROFANITY

Prior to the 1970s, expressions such as "darn," "dang," "son of a gun," "hell's bells," and "shoot" were considered by some to be profane, uncouth in "polite company" and certainly not acceptable in schools.

Instances aplenty have found teachers and students subject to repercussions from their intended or unintended utterances of profanity at school. Many of us teachers choose to delete profane words and gestures from our daily lives, because we *know* that those profanities can too easily slip out during the times we are in school.

Minor incidents like bumping a shin, breaking a piece of equipment, or being startled by an alarm can cause us to let a profanity slip out in front of students. Why risk it? Values and standards for behavior in schools warrant our reaching higher than our colloquial norms and coarse or vulgar language. Our comportment as educators deserves a review of our use of profanity.

Parents have the right to expect professional behaviors from their children's educators. Co-workers have a right to expect it from their colleagues. When teachers use an appropriate range of vocabulary instead of profanity, students have models from which to learn. We can take a few moments to consider the presence of profanity in our in- and out-of-school lives. And some of us may find that our language needs an upgrade.

22 | EMBRACING MISTAKES IN LEARNING

M istakes reveal a lack of learning. Or do they? Possibly they are indicators of *how* to learn.

How do we react when a student makes a mistake? Do we feel frustration? Anger? Disappointment? Do we draw conclusions about the student? "He isn't trying hard enough." "She isn't listening." "He never does his homework." "She doesn't care about being accurate or doing well." "He gives goofy answers on purpose to get attention."

How teachers treat mistakes can make huge differences in students' attitudes toward learning and willingness to learn. Are students eager or hesitant? Do they display perseverance or futility? A wide-eyed "Oops, I made a mistake!" can reveal a very different learning orientation from "I just can't do this!"

What *is* a mistake? A "mis-take" can be the result of so many things: an attention lapse; a motor coordination challenge; mental fatigue; auditory, visual, or motor processing issues; inability to access vocabulary; anxiety over being the center of attention; preoccupation with hunger or worry; fear of judgment. So many possibilities.

If we define learning as a series of "mis-takes" that lead us to accurate, enduring understanding, then we would likely retool our responses to mistakes in the classroom.

Why are we teachers so *bothered* by mistakes? Do we think student mistakes signal our incompetence? Does our frustration assume that students are not trying hard enough?

What would change in our classrooms if we embraced "mis-takes" as valuable, necessary steps toward learning? When we become interested in the mistake rather than the judgment of accuracy, *learning changes. Teaching changes.* With this orientation, mistakes get reframed as mini-discoveries that lead us to what to do next, what to do differently, what to pursue instead.

Teachers who become consumed with detecting mistakes miss some golden opportunities to learn. Imagine teaching a student to shoot free throws on a basketball court, but each time the student shoots, we watch only the basket. It is in watching the shooter, not the basket, that we learn how to teach.

"Student learning is the responsibility of both teachers and students" (Bennett & Bartholomew, 1997, p. 35). When we become curious about mistakes, when we have a healthy eagerness to watch for, analyze, and remedy student errors, we create a shared responsiveness for learning. And we learn together.

23 | ADMINISTRATOR APPRECIATION

Why does it seem so universally fashionable to criticize and distrust administrators? Does their elevated position make them easy targets? Are we ill-informed about the issues and responsibilities of their positions? Do we assume they pursued the position for status, money, and power? Are they ill-informed about *our* teaching specialty?

When asked "Why do you want to be a principal?" administrators are likely to reply with lofty goals: "I want positive change for our kids, teachers, schools, and communities." Sometimes we forget that most school administrators began as classroom educators. And although educators may be frequent critics of administrators, few of us would willingly take their places.

Those leading our schools make decisions constantly, and not all (perhaps very few) decisions can be consultative ones. When conflict arises, leaders can rarely divulge all the information that caused the problem or led to a decision. Sometimes our leaders cannot reveal that *their* administrator gave them no choice in the decision. So there are times when we are not privy to the whole story or a full account of what happened.

Imagine the challenge of being an advocate for all on staff while also taking the responsibility for bringing out and expecting the best from each.

Small gestures of support for your administrator can add to the good feelings within your school. Just as administrators want to bring out the best in us, we can aim to bring out the best in them.

Delivering a handwritten note lends a valued personal touch to supportive feedback.

- "Thank you for making promptness a priority for beginning and concluding our meetings. That is so important to me."
- "I appreciate your compassionate treatment of this family."
- "Thank you for your efforts to make that happen, even though it did not work as well as we thought it would."
- "I appreciate your sensitivity in responding to our colleague. You were a model of diplomacy."
- "The way you explained that thorny issue was a good lesson for all of us."

Most people are a curious contradiction: they desire a dynamic leader to inspire them, and they will also be hostile toward the person who has any power over their destiny. (McGinnis, 1985, p. 155)

24 | MISBEHAVIOR AND BEHAVIOR

Student misbehavior has the power to make our lives miserable, derail our lessons, and convince us that we should not be teachers. Whether we are early-, mid-, or late-career educators, few experiences in life rob us of our peace of mind to the extent that student misbehaviors do.

Sometimes our attempts to manage student behavior problems cause us to become so hypervigilant that we turn into pouncers. We jump on any potential behavioral infraction we see, and that becomes our habit. Always watchful in order to stave off unruly behavior, we can become harsh, unyielding, and strident in our attempts to keep students "under control."

Yet what if we're wrong about misbehavior? What if it's not what we think it is?

One of the most profound changes we can make in our teaching comes from a very simple idea, a unique definition of misbehavior. Educational psychologist C. M. Charles tells us that only when behavior is *knowingly and willingly* obstructing is it *mis*behavior (Charles, 1985, p. 4). Could it be true that most of what we see in schools is simply *behavior*?

Reinterpreting behaviors initially takes some effort, but it is well spent. Soon such reinterpretation becomes automatic. The habit of seeing behavior *first* as simply behavior gives us pause. And that pause allows us to craft our verbal and emotional responses.

- We more often retain a calm internal and external countenance. This calm allows us to address the behavior and the consequence matter-of-factly and without accusation.
- We respond with the appropriate level of assertiveness and direction.
- We give a moment of grace to neutrally identify what we see and hear.
- We explain calmly and assertively why the behavior needs to change.

Consider this. Sometimes we adults are rude, annoying, unfair, rough, or vulgar. Are we misbehaving? Is *our* misbehavior worthy of punishment?

When we give up assuming *intent*, it changes us. We may choose not to ignore the behavior, but we also do not presume malicious or disrespectful intent.

25 | EYE EXPRESSIONS

At times we do not want to show the tension or turmoil we are experiencing. We choose to "save face" with an expression that is best for the situation, but it may differ from what we *feel*. Our intent is not to be disingenuous or manipulative; it is to *give our best* to the encounter.

We rarely get to see our own eye expressions, so we may not know our usual range of expressiveness. The opposites of hard eyes and soft eyes can provide some images.

Hard eyes are squinted, tense, and strongly focused on the target. Often the forehead is creased. Hard eyes portray intensity, anger, frustration, threat, or disagreement, and they do not normally invite interaction. Pain, bright lights, intense thinking, and eye fatigue can cause us to display hard eyes.

Soft eyes are relaxed, rounded, and gently open; the look is thoughtful and inquisitive. Softness can be seen in the skin surrounding the eyes, conveying gentleness, calm, and comfort. Soft eyes are described in martial arts and horse riding as breathing in through your eyes to calm your entire body.

Neutral eyes are mildly focused and reveal no emotion other than attentiveness. More soft than hard, neutral eyes convey an expression that is alert and observant, but perhaps unreadable.

Are you able to identify your habitual eye expressions? Feeling the different eye expressions we display can be key to projecting the messages we want to project. Whether intentional or not, eye expressions can intimidate and demand. They can soothe and support. And they can project unreadable neutrality.

Most of us need to look in a mirror to become familiar with our eye expressions. We need to see and feel the differences as we experiment with hard eyes, soft eyes, and neutral eyes. We need to practice so that we can display eye expressions that do not necessarily match our mood or temper, but do reflect the nonverbal messages we want to send.

The goal of intentional eye expressions is to project the messages we *want* to project. There are times when we want to show what is best for the situation rather than what we are feeling in the moment. As with any other nonverbal behaviors, we benefit from knowing and modifying the messages we send through our eyes.

When we know how to use eye expressions wisely, we can add to the effectiveness of our communications. We can convey our desired responses rather than our reflexive ones. Our students can benefit. Our co-workers can benefit. And we may be more vitally ourselves.

26 | ACKNOWLEDGING BOUNDARIES

We all have boundaries. The limit at which our yes turns to no defines our sense of "crossing the line." Yet others may not have the same lines. Language usage, physical contact, attire, and academic integrity are some of the categories that can incite a sense of boundary violation. Yet we have an obligation to inform. "Knowing and showing" our boundaries can help prevent boundary violations that embarrass and wound.

What boundaries do we take to school? What boundaries do our school policies expect from us? Do we enter school with sensitivities toward others' personal spaces and preferences? Are we careful (full of care) about intruding on others' beliefs and social comfort?

For some, asking personal questions, sharing private information, using profanity, and name-calling cross the lines of acceptability. To function within clear boundaries, we may need to inform others of behavior that makes us uncomfortable. Depending on our level of discomfort, we may need to escalate our responses from cordial conversations to matter-of-fact opinions and eventually to strong "cease and desist" stances.

Choosing an appropriate level of intensity makes clear our expectations for boundaries. If we do not inform others, we cannot justifiably hold them accountable for what they do not know.

When we know our boundaries and when we respect the boundaries of others, we have a much greater chance of properly, sensitively, and comfortably orienting ourselves in schools.

Knowing and living our boundaries develops a healthy trust in ourselves. We need not be haughty or apologetic when we reveal our discomfort with words or behaviors: "I won't cross that line." "I can't be party to this discussion." "I'm exceedingly uncomfortable with this conversation." "She has a right to expect that conversation to be kept private." "I believe there are some ethical issues to be considered with this situation."

Dubious behaviors can too easily become unexamined habits. Once a state of mutual trust is breached, returning to that state can take time, effort, and commitment. Knowing and showing school-appropriate boundaries can help everyone.

27 | COOPERATION IN THE CLASSROOM

When we aim to teach students how to cooperate and assist others, we shift students' focus to self-satisfaction and collaborative support. To fully appreciate this shift, it can be helpful to consider some differences between competition and cooperation.

Alfie Kohn tells us that *structural competitions* are contests that require one's failure for another's success. *Intentional competition* occurs when we purposely set up mini-competitions to see who will win. These competitions may focus on attire, attractiveness, being first on the bus, having the nicest home, and so on. When structural competition coats our habits of mind, we can unknowingly develop tendencies toward intentional competition: we constantly judge who is better or worse. Our sense of accomplishment is often only momentary (Kohn, 1992, pp. 4–5).

Learning the skills of cooperation could be an antidote to the drawbacks of competition for our students, but such goals need not be systematized. Simple, consistent acknowledgments of cooperation can inform and facilitate throughout classroom activities.

- "I'm interested in hearing your observations, not your evalua-tions of classmates' efforts."
- "Check with your partner about his or her idea before you tell me what you think."
- "Our reward for meeting all those challenges is the feeling within us. Can you feel it?"
- "In this lesson, you need to consider yourselves thinkers, not winners." (Bennett & Bartholomew, 1997, p. 204).

28 | CLEANING UP CLUTTER

How messy *are* our lives at school? Sometimes the internal and external clutter steals our peace of mind, and we feel like hoarders in our own classrooms. At times, a good cleanup is just what we need to make a fresh start, renew our energy, and create a hopeful outlook.

Look around. Is the desk overflowing with "stuff"? Are walls devoid of graphics, furniture in disarray, relationships strained, lessons falling flat, encounters with administrators more about resistance than openness?

Look inside. Are you constantly ruminating about difficulties that seem never to be resolved? Is there ill will festering against students, faculty, parents, or administrators?

If you're feeling the clutter, the metaphoric "kitchen sink" cleanup may be just what is needed (Carroll, 2006). We begin by taking a first, strategic step toward cleaning the mess.

If we walk into a dirty, messy kitchen, starting the cleaning process can feel overwhelming. Yet if we clean and prepare the sink *first*, we create a space for *continuing* to clean. One clean and tidy space gives us incentive to clean the rest of the kitchen. We see details previously unnoticed. We sort and put away. We may be eager to cook again. We feel optimism about possibilities for the future. We are more welcoming to guests. We feel more broadly reoriented in the world.

What is *your* kitchen sink? Whether physical, personal, or social, finding and cleaning up your clutter can give you a new start. And taking those steps shows "a profound respect for the world . . . [B]eing precise and thorough and fresh . . . is the natural thing to do" (Carroll, 2006, p. 98).

29 | STAY YOU

One of the most important features of a treadmill is that *we* get to push the buttons. *We* choose to go faster or slower. *We* raise or lower the incline. *We* determine how much we are able to accomplish at any given time.

Imagine that you have a treadmill in the hallway outside your room at school. Every time *anyone* walks down the hall, he or she can push *any* button on your treadmill. At any moment, you may be forced to walk or run, go up an incline or down. You may be forced to stop abruptly or run to the point of exhaustion. You may have a painful injury or medical condition unknown to others, but that does not influence the rigorous choices others make for you.

This imaginary scenario is, of course, a metaphor for how we can be pulled out of ourselves and how we can allow others to mismanage us. Those who push our buttons do so with our tacit permission. At some level, we allow it.

Being savvy about the metaphoric treadmills in schools means that we are sensitive to our own needs and knowledgeable about our own capacities. We can stay *us*. We can reclaim the best of us.

We must divest ourselves from others who, intentionally or unintentionally, take control over us. Simply removing ourselves from the situation is sometimes best. Speaking up can clarify needs. Staying silent can allow us to resolve the matter without letting others know our struggle. Decide whether speaking up or choosing a silent solution is better for you. Stay you.

> Any time you can demonstrate your willingness to listen to someone with a minimum of self-defensiveness or criticism, you are cultivating virtues within yourself that have a high payoff in self-respect. Any significant personal change requires exactly this kind of courage: the willingness to feel uncomfortable while acting "as if" one is more mature and capable than one's familiar self. (Rusk 1993, 70)

30 | FIVE QUESTIONS

Sometimes when we are in a frenzy or down in the dumps, we just need a little perspective. Any problem can benefit from perspective.

Asking ourselves five simple questions can help determine the import of an issue:

- Will this be important five minutes from now?
- Will this be important five hours from now?
- Will this be important five weeks from now?
- Will this be important five months from now?
- Will this be important five years from now?

The heft of conflicts and the gravity of decision-making can seem overwhelming. Giving ourselves a "five questions" check can help restore our perspective and decisiveness . . . and therefore our peaceful state of mind.

31 | FEEDBACK THAT FEEDS

Ask yourself this question: "What do I want students to believe about themselves when they are in my presence?"

When we orient ourselves with this question, it shapes our responsiveness to students. We use words that grow rather than wither, that offer instructive comments rather than give general praise, and that give direction for correction and improvement. We *feed learning* by utilizing informed, instructional, purposeful feedback.

Is your feedback too general to be instructional? "Wonderful!" "Terrific!" "Good work." "Try harder." "That's not it." Sometimes we can get caught in the dichotomy of delivering either praise or criticism. Praise can be nearly as perilous as criticism. Superiority, inferiority, resentment, and embarrassment are some of the potential side effects of praising students. Empty praise can also become habitual ("Very good!") and feel manipulative ("You're so good at that, would you do this for me?").

Some who work with students ask, "How does that make you feel?" This is such a personal question, and it should not substitute for asking "What did you learn from that?" or saying "That must feel so satisfying!" It may not be our business to ask or know how others feel, and it does not focus on the problem-solving nature of learning. Other statements to use instead are: "What are you thinking about that?" "How would you describe your dilemma?" "What do you plan to do next?"

When we become adept at observational feedback, we open a wide range of additional possibilities. We watch and listen to students, then construct instructional feedback to support their learning. If praise is used, it is most often paired with specific feedback.

- "Based on what I'm seeing, this may be confusing for you right now. Is that what you think?"
- "Your ideas just seem to bubble up, Emile. But keep them inside now so I can listen to Joshua."
- "What puzzles you about that? I appreciate how you can zero in on the problem."
- "That was about 90 percent accurate. Do you have a sense of how you could make it 100 percent?"
- "Appropriate vocabulary. Clear explanation. Solid problem-solving. You figured it out!"

[Children] need to know that they are valued for themselves, not merely to the degree to which they meet our expectations or follow our rules. (McGinnis, 1985, p. 113)

32 | PERSONALITY PREFERENCES

Each of us likely has mild to strong preferences for certain personalities. And those personalities may or may not be similar to our own.

Given the sometimes powerful reactions to personalities in schools, it may be worth thinking about them and considering their influence on us.

- A teacher relies on sarcastic humor for interacting with teachers and students. Some like the teasing. Others find it offensive.
- A teacher is demure and quiet. Some appreciate the calm. Others distrust the lack of responsiveness to co-workers.
- A principal is very efficient and responsible in managing school issues, yet teachers and parents feel slighted by an assumed lack of interest in them.
- A principal is so generous, affectionate, and outgoing that teachers begin to wish for a strong disciplinarian, rather than a grandparent figure.

Whether we are drawn to or repelled by certain personalities, we are likely to face them in schools. And it is to our advantage to both notice our personality preferences and actively coach ourselves to *look* and *behave* beyond them, instead of letting them interfere with our teaching or our collegiality.

Exuberant personalities. Quiet personalities. Which do you prefer as friends? Which do you prefer as students?

All ages of people, from preschool on, could have personalities that repel or ignite our sense of comfort and affinity. This is common, and it is normal. *How we act* on those feelings, however, can affect the health of our relationships and the effectiveness of our teaching.

No matter the level of exuberance or quietness, we would be remiss to gauge expertise, leadership, or friendliness by the magnitude of others' social behaviors. Plus it can be important for us to notice when our own quietness or liveliness has a dampening effect on our teaching, conversations, and group discussions.

Personalities can push us away or draw us near. We benefit when we treat a person (including a student or teacher) openly and kindly regardless of our initial, instinctive, emotional response to that individual's personality.

Greatness is in having a purpose—not in just having a personality. (Hifler, 1992, p. 164)

33 | THE VIRTUE OF LISTENING

In schools, we listen. We listen to discoveries. We listen to tensions. We listen to revelations. Listening informs us about others and about ourselves. At the heart of teaching, there is listening.

How good are we at listening? Do we give the speaker our full attention? Some of us specialize in distracted listening. We veer off course. We drift as we "listen" to a student telling us about his important news. We plan our lesson as we "listen" to lunchroom talk. We craft our rebuttal as we "listen" to someone disagreeing with us.

As with so many other behaviors, our listening can have wide ranges of intensity. We can become so absorbed in our school duties that we develop a habit of *not* listening.

Often, it seems, listening becomes a casualty of multitasking: "listening" as we grade papers, read an announcement, straighten our room. Yet news has also reached us that multitasking may not be as desirable as or effective as we think. When do we still our minds and bodies to *just listen*?

- When a student expresses frustration in completing an assignment or learning task, gently "ask, listen, and learn" about the obstacle she is facing.
- When a parent is worried about his child's behavior, "ask, listen, and learn" to best formulate your compassionate response.
- When a committee is at odds about projected changes, set the tone by "asking, listening, and learning" to further the goals of mutual, respectful problem-solving.

When we infuse our schools with active listening and responsive commentary, we upgrade our levels of vitality and vigor. We supplant the detached "surface listening" with active, quizzical listening that provides real communication, real connection.

As an experiment, devote one day to attentive, focused listening at school. Notice what happens on your "listening day."

Any time you can demonstrate your willingness to listen to someone with a minimum of self-defensiveness or criticism, you are cultivating virtues within yourself that have a high payoff in self-respect. (Rusk, 1993, p. 70)

34 | MUSICALITY IN EVERY SUBJECT

Expressiveness, flow, and emotion, make music charming, appealing, and moving. Those manifestations are what make music an art. They are what make music *musical*. When music is stripped of its musicality in order to study it, we can lose the very aesthetic that makes it worthy of listening, performing, and studying (Bennett, 2016). The same is true for nearly any other school subject.

Passion for a subject and desire to share that passion are likely what motivated us to become teachers. It should be no surprise, then, that the quality of the subject matter in our classrooms can influence our vitality for teaching and students' vitality for learning.

Sometimes it is our quest to teach information *about* our subject that diminishes the very qualities that inspire our passion *for* it. What a paradox: the way we teach a subject can cause students to lose interest in learning it! How does this happen?

Prioritizing expressiveness and curiosity can revitalize us. When we strip enjoyment and fascination from learning and focus only on mechanics or information, we may be strangling interest and aesthetic appeal for our students *and* for ourselves. What can we do?

- *Create* lessons that capture students' interest in learning. Find "hooks" that catch their curiosity.
- *Immerse* students in a subject's applicability to and connections with their daily lives.
- *Infuse* lessons with quirky or humorous samples of ways the subject can be understood or used.

Passion for any subject, the musicality of it, can be ignited or extinguished in schools. Teaching subjects in lifeless ways can wear on *our* spirits. Let's give ourselves permission to highlight aspects of our subjects we enjoy and commit ourselves to teaching those subjects with integrity. When we teach what we love and love what we teach, we are vibrant . . . and so is learning.

35 | CONFLICT HAPPENS

Conflict is a way of life. Many of us, from the days of our youth, have developed habits to avoid conflict. By agreeing, apologizing, and pretending, we can sidestep many of the conflicts that come our way. But these coping behaviors are not necessarily healthy for us or for those on the other side of the conflict.

What if we were able to see conflicts (large and small) as opportunities to problem-solve? "The key mistake we make when we feel frustrated is to abandon the problem-solving game and turn to the power game instead" (Ury, 1993, p. 132). How might our days in school be different if we were able to dissolve conflicts maturely and respectfully? Momentary discomforts quickly shift to momentary reflection. Conflict converts to an opportunity to learn and grow, rather than shrink and cower.

When conflict is focused on transforming people (including ourselves) and not just changing situations, the results are bigger than resolution. Our disputes become a "supremely important human enterprise [that] embodies and expresses the highest and best within us as human beings" (Bush and Folger, 1994, p. 83).

When we do not run from conflict, we begin to see and feel it as a necessary part of life. When conflict no longer frightens us, we stay calm in the face of anger. We allow time to simply consider rather than fix. We breathe our way into self-assurance.

With our new lens, we give conflict a more balanced interpretation, a more reasoned response. We do not perseverate; we deny ourselves the "worry habit." We move through the dilemma. We let it be, inhaling and exhaling, to get ourselves back to a stance of strength and wisdom.

> Value conflict as a positive, seeing it as an adventure or journey, an opportunity for growth and change, an invitation to intimacy and relationship, and an opening for transformation. (Bowling & Hoffmann, 2003, p. 54)

36 | FREEZING IMAGES

Can you envision yourself in this scene?

> I saw her disdain for me pasted like an announcement on her forehead. She must have heard that I made some critical remarks about her presentation. Her icy treatment makes it clear that she is distancing herself from me. I veer off down another hallway to avoid her.

We freeze images when we assume that a past encounter with someone is as foremost in their minds as it is in ours. The episode may have been recent or from the distant past. Yet we believe our awkwardness, anger, or warmth is as prevalent in the other's mind as it is in ours.

We think the warm smile signals that he remembers the wonderful conversation we had. That the grumpy look means she is still unhappy about my declining that invitation. That the chilliness in his greeting means he still resents my publicly challenging his opinion.

Fairly often, however, the person we have been avoiding *may not even recall the encounter*! The scowl or warmth we see aimed at us may have nothing to do with us! And it may not even be a scowl that we are seeing!

Conjuring intent, good and bad, where there is none can become a habit. And the only way to clear the air is to communicate, to ask.

- "Am I sensing correctly that you feel awkward toward me because of our dispute at the meeting?"
- "My memory of that argument still makes me uncomfortable. Can we talk about it?"
- "By the way you were smiling and contributing to the discussion, you seemed in agreement with the points I was making. Am I interpreting that correctly?"

Freedom is what we are after. Dispelling our own limiting beliefs releases and revitalizes us. Learning that we were wrong about our negative assumptions can bring about euphoria. Thawing those frozen images can reset us on a path of vibrancy in our school relationships.

37 | THE TOLL OF DISRUPTIONS

"This job is driving me crazy . . . literally!" Spoken by a frenzied educator, these words testify to the many disruptions that happen in schools. The fast pace of our myriad daily experiences can cause our thoughts to disconnect, our minds to overload, our brains to feel like they are on the verge of explosion.

We remember the time a fight broke out in class and we had to stop it. We remember the time the principal punished our student (without our knowledge) for a minor infraction. We remember the time a child vomited on our new shoes and we had to wear them the remainder of the day.

These are the standout episodes. The disruptions are certainly memorable, and they can make for good-natured storytelling.

According to Jones, however, the toll of these big moments of disruption pales in comparison to the smaller ones. Both common and constant, small disruptions erode our patience and rob our peace of mind. Like the constant drip of a faucet or hum of a motor, it is the underlying persistence of sound and motion that can zap our energy and compromise our endurance.

Are we aware of or immune to the low levels of noise and disarray in our classes? Are our students? While perhaps not warranting punishment or disciplinary action, small disruptions may be subliminal, but they are powerful. For the vitality of our students and ourselves, noting the impact of small interruptions may be worth a look, a listen, and a resolution.

> The most persistent *misconception* about discipline is that the most important problems in discipline management are the biggest problems, the crises. Certainly they are the most memorable. When teachers look back over the year, they will certainly remember the time the fight broke out or the time a student told them to do an unnatural act . . . . The most important and costly type of discipline problem in any classroom is the *small disruption* . . . . Ironically, therefore, the most important discipline problem in the classroom is the small disruption, not the crisis. It is the small disruption by its very *frequency* that destroys the teacher's patience by degrees and destroys learning by the minute. (Jones, 1987, pp. 27–28)

38 | HURTING IN SCHOOLS

Acknowledging the role we play in hurting can be uncomfortable. Whether the hurt is being done by us or being done to us, we play a role in allowing it.

Our words and deeds can cause hurt (and often residual anger) whether or not we intend it. Words commonly used in our homes and social groups may sound harsh and insulting to co-workers, administrators, students, and parents. To our ears, those words may sound harmless, but to others, they may feel harmful.

Are we accountable for others' reactions to our behaviors? To an extent, yes, we are. Are we responsive to acknowledging our role in hurting? Likely the answer is sometimes yes, sometimes no.

Schools flow with actions and reactions. We all have responsibilities for making the layers of communication work.

When we get hurt, our reactions to the offense often make matters worse. As in a football game, we take positions of offense or defense and then choose our next play.

- *We evade*, pretending we're not hurt. But we carry around the unresolved resentment. And sometimes the resentment festers rather than fades.
- *We punish*, shunning the offenders with the silent treatment. But sometimes they don't notice. And sometimes the vengeful thoughts hurt us more than them.
- *We tattle*, exaggerating just enough so listeners will be as indignant as we are.
- *We confront* the offender, yet angry accusations solve little or nothing.

When we do the hurting, we may tell ourselves, "She had it coming" or "I'm giving him some of his own medicine." But lowering ourselves to poor behavior does little to right the wrongs of being hurt.

For every human encounter, even those ridden with conflict, we have choices. Shut down or open up. Connect or disconnect. Hold on or let go. Make peace or make hostility. Mend or rend. Which do we choose?

> Negative states of mind . . . destroy our mental happiness. Once you harbor feelings of hatred or ill feeling toward someone, once you yourself are filled by hatred or negative emotions, then other people appear to you as also hostile. (Dalai Lama & Cutler, 1998, p. 39)

39 | MY WORD!

Name-calling and use of offensive words appear to be increasingly acceptable in our communities and in our entertainment venues. Offensive words have no place in schools. Yet how do we know what is offensive, especially across diversities of age, family values, and ethnicity? We can become immune to commonly used expletives, even when teachers hold themselves to a higher standard than the general public.

The intent in questioning some words and sayings here is twofold: to make us aware of our sometimes automatic responses and to encourage attention to and reconsideration of words and phrases we may be using in schools.

- *Inflammatory words* may be so commonly overused that they lose their shock effect: "loser," "jerk," "bully," "predator," "troublemaker," "dumb," "harasser," "racist." Nonetheless, name-calling is risky, hurtful, and confrontational.
- *Slogans and sayings* that at one time were novel and clever can be overused and lose their potency. When phrases become too repetitive and too predictable, students can be repelled by them rather than attentive to them. One example was a

junior high school principal who, during every school assembly, would step to the microphone and drone, "We're waiting on you!" The too-predictable admonition was rarely, if ever, effective. Other examples could be "Crisscross applesauce" when we want students to sit cross-legged on the floor, "I'm the teacher, you're the listener," and "No pain, no gain."

- *Offensive words* can sometimes be defused by probing a bit about what a student or teacher means: "What does that word mean?" "Can you tell me why you're using that word?" "That word produces a strong reaction in me."

It is natural and valuable to react to language. We can hardly prevent it. It is our primary and primal avenue for communication. Yet it is good for us as teachers to pay attention. It is smart to reflect on the meaning and the impacts of the words we say and hear. It is wise to be informed and purposeful with our vocabulary in schools.

40 | CONTEXT EFFECT

Comparing ourselves to other teachers can be deflating and discouraging. Yet who *doesn't* do it?

We notice her mutually warm relationships with students. We see his students' stellar accomplishments at the science fair. We wonder how our team leader is able to help her students achieve the reading acumen they demonstrate. We envy the way the coach is able to tame even the most explosive tempers.

Even though envy is troublesome, comparing ourselves *too favorably* to others is not the answer, either. The high is always temporary.

The effect of context can hardly be overstated. And "context appropriateness" suggests that we recognize and adapt our expectations to the important differences in context that affect learning. *Context can be an even more powerful influence on learning than age or development.*

Sometimes subtle and sometimes blatant, differences in the attributes listed here influence both our teaching and students' learning.

Physical attributes: class size, room size, room shape, room
temperature, amount of equipment available, seating
space and type, relative clutter or tidiness in room

Temporal attributes: time of day, time of year, frequency and
length of class meeting, interval between instructional
times, classes or events directly preceding or following
our lessons

Teacher attributes: familiarity with students and community,
number of classes and subjects taught per day, length of
time in same school, years of experience teaching, access
to professional development and mentoring

Student attributes: familiarity with classmates, mix of
characteristics (gender, ethnicity, language, economic
status, age, special needs or exceptions), general interest
and investment in learning

Community/school attributes: administrative and collegial
respect and support, performance expectations, parental
participation, community involvement and advocacy
(Bennett & Bartholomew, 1997)

Rebalancing views of ourselves and others based on the varying
attributes of our teaching settings can ground healthy, realistic
expectations. And that vibrant health can steer us toward reasonable professional goals and relationships.

41 | LEAVE IT!

"Leave it" is one of the first commands to teach a dog, for its own protection and the protection of others. Oddly, the concept is one that may be a good fit for harried teachers as well.

Envision a time when you may have benefited from pausing and saying to yourself, "Leave it":

- Staying at school after hours to continue working, even when your brainpower is low, your energy has tanked, and you need rest.
- Ruminating over an incident that continues to worry you because you are not sure how to interpret a comment made by your principal.
- Feeling frazzled after witnessing a verbal confrontation that began as a simple disagreement but evolved into a hostile exchange.

At times it can be beneficial to compartmentalize our minds and emotions. In fact, if we are not able to sift and rank our priorities, we can be in nearly constant turmoil. "One thing at a time" may be an impossible goal for a teacher. Yet saying "leave it" and giving our trouble some distance (even momentarily) can be an important strategy for mental health and teacher effectiveness.

Some of us tend to be ruminators, chewing our cud, swallowing it, bringing it back up, and chewing it again. Although it may keep us busy, rumination can be a form of self-torture, getting us nowhere.

When we tell ourselves to "leave it," we know we are thought-stopping for a good cause. We are taking some moments to release, relax, and regroup. We are letting go long enough to revive.

> It isn't a matter of trying harder or giving more. Frequently, something doesn't click into place until we turn it loose and walk away. The release is not to accept defeat but it is saying we have done what we can and now we will stand and let it work. (Hifler, 1992, p. 311)

42 | TEACHERS BEING FRIENDLY

The ease of school relationships can wax and wane just as in any other group. When teachers get along well, the entire school can be a vibrantly productive and nourishing environment. When teachers have conflicts, chilliness and fragmented collegiality can affect everyone.

Why would we expect teachers to be happily cooperative all the time? Teachers likely do not have a hand in hiring their co-workers, and therefore they must adjust to all types of personalities, pedagogical preferences, and teaching styles. Even with these sometimes strident differences, collegial relationships are essential to the health of schools and school personnel.

Key to this vision is behaving with friendliness to others, rather than expecting all others to be our friends. When the "Be friendly, but not friends" mantra is given to student teachers and school interns, it is intended to help these novice educators maintain professional distances with students. But for teachers at any stage of their career, it also can be helpful to distinguish friendship and friendliness.

We could define "friends" as:

- Those with whom we spend time outside school hours
- Those who know our family and home life
- Those with whom we share personal, sometimes private information

Using these criteria, we may have more acquaintances than friends at school. And those professional distances are not necessarily a hindrance to vibrant school communities.

With courteous conversations, cordial comportment, and caring camaraderie, being friend*ly* may be enough.

43 | SELF-TALK

The voice we hear most often throughout our lives is our own. Whether in whispers or roars, silence or resound, our self-talk is nearly constant, even when we try not to listen.

Compliments, encouragement, reassurance. Insults, accusations, disapproval. We sometimes do not notice the ongoing chatter inside our heads, but it is there. So beware. Self-talk may be the most perennial tool for self-inflicting toxic and diminishing thoughts. And, unfortunately, the hurtful and demeaning judgments seem to live on in us . . . *because* we continue to repeat them to ourselves. *We* keep our hurt alive.

One word, phrase, or sentence is spoken to us, and we continue repeating it to ourselves, long after the initial speaker is gone. The echoes of hurtful words have long life spans, *if we allow them.*

Self-talk can also speak to us of kind, reassuring and strengthening thoughts. Our self-talk can bolster us. Listen. Consider. Reconstruct. Enlist your voice to acknowledge, support, and affirm the best of you.

- *Beware* what we tell ourselves about any given situation. We can choose our narrative.
- *Pay attention* to the persevering voices inside us. Dismantle the destructive ones. Cultivate the strengthening ones.
- *Choose our inner dialogue.* We have the power of choice.

44 | JUST BREATHE

"Just breathe." Two very potent words. We may hear them when we are anxious or fretting. We may silently speak them when we yearn for tranquility.

In and out . . . the power of that simple practice of breathing is palpable. Breathe in slowly through your nose to gather strength, wisdom, and calm. Breathe out slowly through your mouth to release weakness, confusion, and threat.

The power of breath offers calm and restores vigor in ways large and small.

- Breathing can dissipate and dissolve apprehension.
- Breathing can muster our best intentions.
- Breathing can project our voices without harshness or stridency.
- Breathing can create soft eyes that project calm.
- Breathing can shift frenzy to composure.
- Breathing can give us the calm that we need to choose our responses carefully.
- Breathing can reinvigorate our mind and spirit.

You feel nervous before teaching a new lesson about which you are not fully confident. Just breathe. You are summoned to speak to the principal about a thorny issue involving another teacher, and you are worried about what to say. Just breathe. A parent stridently lets you know that your teaching does not measure up to his expectation. Just breathe.

When you need to summon your strongest rather than your most vulnerable self, just breathe.

Though chest breathing has now become natural and involuntary for most of us, it is really a part of the fight/flight syndrome, aroused when the organism is challenged by some external stress or danger. Because of the reciprocity between breath and mind, chest breathing, in turn, gives rise to the tension and anxiety associated with fight/flight syndrome. With chest breathing, the breath is shallow, jerky and unsteady, resulting in similar unsteadiness of the mind. All techniques aimed at providing relaxation of the body, nerves and mind will be ineffective unless chest breathing is replaced by deep, even and steady diaphragmatic breathing. (Rama, Ballentine, and Hymes, 1979, p. 109)

45 | BEING LIKED

- What happens when we believe someone likes us? Do we find ourselves seeing the best qualities in that person as a result?
- What happens when we believe someone dislikes us? Do we find ourselves looking for qualities to dislike in that person?
- To what extent is our sense of well-being in schools dependent on our students, colleagues, staff, administrators, and parents liking us?

Whether we are right or wrong about being liked, intense susceptibility to another's opinion can surrender our power and rob us of our peace of mind. When we regularly feed our need to be liked, the craving often becomes insatiable, and any fulfillment becomes temporary.

Envision a person saying, "I don't like you," and you lightheartedly replying (and *meaning*), "That's okay." When we are able to say, and mean, "That's okay," we feel a sense of strength and solid grounding. We allow that person's feelings and issues to *stay with him*. We allow that person her opinion, but we do not adopt it as our own. We do not fret about the "liking."

In schools, a "like addiction" can be costly to healthy environments: it makes us fragile and needy. How do we get rid of it? Taking inventory of our own habits can be a first step.

1. *Avoid ruminating over faults.* It makes them grow bigger. A criticism made by one person can cause us to wonder if others think the same. We can convince ourselves that "everyone knows" and "everyone is judging me." Worry over weaknesses can be paralyzing. The attitude "I can fix this" moves us through our doubt as we aim to improve.
2. *Beware of strategies we use to get others to like us.* Empty compliments, aversions to disagreement, and eagerness to alleviate discomfort potentially rob us of necessary growth and social rebalancing.
3. *Be beneficent, not pandering, in responses to others.* Offer goodwill because it is best for someone, not to solicit that person's good opinion of us.

When our need to be liked is prominent, we think too shallowly. Someone smiles; he likes us. Someone doesn't invite us to a social event; she doesn't like us. We receive a thank-you note from a parent; he likes us. Being liked can be highly overrated, especially when it becomes a need.

When we hitch our star to the "like me" wagon, we are doomed to be a victim who is never satisfied for long. Instead, focus on being a compassionate, strongly oriented, well-informed educator. Shift behavioral and emotional focus to contributing to the health and goodwill of students and teachers, parents and principals. Teaching with vitality depends on devoting our efforts to the health of ourselves and our school communities.

46 | DOWNSHIFTING

When we are driving a car and shift to a lower gear, we cause the engine to downshift. Sometimes we can hear and feel the drag on the motor as the engine slows the car. As we feel the mechanical tug slowing us down, momentum lags.

Description of an engine downshifting is an excellent parallel for what happens in our brains when we confront fear, fatigue, and confusion. Why is downshifting so important to consider? In schools, teachers and students can experience downshifting multiple times a day. A problem overwhelms. Criticism and embarrassment threaten. Fear looms.

Downshifting happens in our brains as a tug to slow down. Especially when we experience threat or fear, our brains' reactions get primal. As Hart describes it, the primordial slowdown allows us to conserve energy. It is our brain's way of preparing to fight or flee, readying to attack or run. The fight-or-flight response activates unless we can mitigate the fear (Hart, 1983, p. 108).

In schools, both teachers and students can feel as if they are perpetually in fight-or-flight mode. When we are tense, angry, or paranoid, our brains do not allow us to calmly or efficiently learn, absorb, or retain. When threat is present, "full use of the . . . cerebral brain is suspended, and the faster acting, simpler brain resources take larger roles" (Hart, 1983, p. 108).

The concept of downshifting can help us be attuned to and wary of the toll that threat takes on learning and functioning. Shutting down or slowing our cognitive functions during a downshift can cause loss of memory, attention, and concentration. Vitality, calm, and openness are casualties of such a state, for both teachers and students.

Investing ourselves in eliminating (or minimizing) fear from our classrooms, hallways, and lunchrooms serves a great purpose for our learners. Safety and security allow interest and concentration. With conscious efforts to stimulate curiosity, inspire effort, and encourage achievement, all while providing safety, the boosts in learning (and teaching) can be exponential.

47 | CONFIDENTIALITY FOR OTHERS

In schools, we are privy to information about students, teachers, parents, support staff, administrators, and community members. What are our responsibilities in having such information?

Most of us have had to be taught the parameters of confidentiality. And some of us have not had those teachings. For healthy schools, it is imperative for us to protect others' personal, private information and behaviors.

But confidentiality is not as simple as it seems. Although it feels good to talk about ourselves with co-workers, occasionally relationships cool and the closeness that at one time felt secure is no longer an alliance. It is normal and not uncommon for school friendships to go awry. And when relationships diminish or sour, we still need to see and work with those people every day, no matter how awkward that may be.

Confidences once shared in private and then divulged to others are rarely retold with the same words, inflections, or contexts as the originals. If we know that our revelations about home or school life will likely, perhaps unintentionally, be misrepresented, would that change our sense of what to divulge and what not to in schools?

Unfettered openness about our personal opinions and activities, whether shared in or out of schools, can typecast us. Hearing an appalling revelation can (often too easily) override another's views of our expertise, commitment, and character.

Teaching is such an honorable profession, and it asks us to behave honorably. Whether it is maintaining confidentiality about ourselves or about others, we choose wisely what we do and what we share. When we set such boundaries, we can feel invigorated by our own stance, our own social wisdom.

48 | THE ART OF REPRIMAND

Reprimanding students may be a necessary part of teaching. But is there a way to do so *artfully*?

We search for publications in which authors give specific ways to think about and react to student behaviors. We find an approach that fits our temperament, our school's expectations, and the community's sensitivities.

Yet one approach does not fit *all* teachers, or *all* students. As you consult others' recommendations, be open to considering both softer and harder approaches for your reprimands. We all need a *range* to be effective. Add to your options; expand your pool of choices.

A sliding scale of reprimands that adapts to varying degrees of gravity is worth developing. An artful scold has the capacity to serve both teachers and students. And when we are confident that our reprimands are not overly harsh, not overly meek, and definitely not demeaning, we develop the calm and trustful feelings of a vitally grounded teacher.

As a brief and specific formula for the art of reprimand, try these four steps (McGinnis, 1985, p. 62):

1. Do it immediately.
2. Confirm the facts; be sure your information is correct.
3. Be very specific in telling the other person what is wrong. Try to criticize her behavior, not her motives.
4. Show your feelings: anger, annoyance, frustration.

> We will never be able to manage and motivate if we are afraid to correct people's mistakes . . . . If we are going to enforce high standards it will require us to tell people when they do not meet those standards. (McGinnis, 1985, p. 62)

49 | PITFALLS OF ASSUMING

Assumptions we make multiple times a day about others in our schools are necessary. Yet they also warrant a caveat. Assumptions can create a world of misjudgments and misery.

When we make ourselves vulnerable to others' behaviors, and when we believe our interpretations of what happened and why, we can become victims of our own suspicions . . . especially when our conclusions are not accurate. Such oppressive assumptions cause us unrest and snuff out our vitality for being the teacher we want to be.

1. *Team members laugh and talk as a group, but don't include us.* "They don't invite me to join them. I don't belong."
2. *A parent of our student is especially friendly with a co-worker.* "He prefers that teacher over me."
3. *Our principal frequently asks the opinion of a co-worker, but never us.* "She doesn't see me as a leader in this school."

Have you noticed how easy it is to create an entire scenario based on one brief, chance encounter? Some of us are experts at story-making when we see others behaving in ways that we think reflect on us. If we do not stop this kind of assuming, we live at the whim of others' behaviors and our own imaginations. And when we are in this mode of assuming, we often compare our insides to others' outsides.

Our imaginations and suppositions can rule us. And we can get so mixed up in assuming we know another's intentions that we forget to question our own. Develop a propensity for pondering. Placing a *membrane of wisdom* between us and others in schools can be a gift to us and to them.

The next time we make an assumption about a person's mood, intent, word choice, or friendliness, we can stop and think of two reasons our assumption could be wrong.

- "They didn't know that we wanted to be included in the shared, lighthearted moment."
- "We didn't know that the parent and teacher work together on a neighborhood project."
- "We didn't know that the principal and teacher took a course together about the issue being addressed."

We are in charge of our thoughts and assumptions. And since we have a choice, we can assume the best of someone, the worst, or neither. Vitality is regained with we learn and practice ways to be generous of spirit, assertively communicative, and solidly grounded in wisdom and goodwill.

50 | TIME TO BEWARE

When we are vulnerable, it's time to be extra cautious. Physically or emotionally, there are times when we know we are not at our best. We may be in pain, fatigued, fearful, or just out of sorts. It is a "beware time."

Imagine yourself at your best, descending a set of stairs. You hop from step to step. You move quickly and confidently. You don't even *look* at the steps. You don't hold on to the banister. You are extremely confident and efficient.

Now imagine yourself injured or in pain as you descend a set of stairs. You are cautious. You cling unsteadily to the banister for support. You move slowly, placing both feet on one step before you move to the next. You are tense as you hold tightly to the person you have asked to assist you. You don't take your eyes off the danger, looking at nothing but the steps you need to traverse. You use all your diminished strength to keep from falling. Your heart is racing.

We all have occasions to experience confident freedom and cautious fear. Like navigating the stairs when we are impaired, we need to *know* when we are especially vulnerable.

Vulnerability can cloud our awareness and distract our attention. We can be prone to losing our patience, our temper, our composure. We follow a protocol for protecting a physical injury; protecting our spirit can be just as important.

Our vulnerabilities wax and wane. Being aware helps us move into caution mode for a time, taking care to protect ourselves until it passes.

Acknowledging your own "beware time" can be like wrapping yourself in a layer of protective padding or using a periscope to check out any risks hiding in the periphery. Your "beware time" may pass quickly or may amount to nothing. But naming it and being extra gentle with yourself can be a nice oasis of self-care and self-knowledge.

51 | TWO-WORD CUES

In classrooms, many of our words are extraneous. Haven't we all had the experience of listening to someone use so many words to explain that we lose interest and discipline to listen?

Brevity can be powerful. Two-word cues can help us be concise, direct, and specific (Bennett, 2010, p. 3): "Voices ready." "Eyes here." "Sitting tall." "Lips closed." "Hands quiet." "Ears ready." "Breath energy." "No sound." "Pencils down." "Not now."

No matter the age, these kinds of cues are clear and brief. Even if repetition of the two-word directive is needed, the brevity has power.

When students are accustomed to hearing brief instructions, a one-word direction can work just as well: "Ears . . ." "Eyes . . ." Hands . . ." "Tall . . ." "Breathe . . ."

With economy of language comes several benefits. Fewer words mean (1) more focus, less distraction while listening for the key directions, (2) more rest for our voices during a busy teaching day, (3) more moments of attentive silence during lessons, and (4) more simplicity for those who struggle with language processing.

Two-word cues can be assertive in order to get students' attention. Yet our intonation and inflection need not be commanding or scolding. Cues are often more effective when they are not.

Spoken with the intonation of a reminder, a simple statement, or a cordial request, two-word cues can give the message of courteous elicitation. The power of brevity is a simple yet profound idea. Try it. Notice effects. Good luck.

52 | RANKISM IN SCHOOLS

"Rankism," as Fuller describes it, may not be a critical problem in schools. Yet some could benefit from knowing this "ism" and how it can manifest itself and destabilize relationships. As an assertion of superiority, rankism can be subtle or blatant and can serve as a framework to explain some behaviors that feel dominating or oppressive.

- A co-worker treats his number of years teaching as license to prevail in making decisions about school practices.
- A principal makes a unilateral decision without consulting the teachers it will affect.
- Teachers behave with aloofness toward custodial teams and administrative assistants.

Though perhaps subtle, each of these three events can send the message "I outrank you. So do what I say."

Imagine a scene where students are leaving your class. As you stand at the door, students file out. You stop Samuel, who has had chronic behavior challenges. "You were much better behaved today, Samuel. I'm proud of your improvement." The next day, as the same class is leaving your room, Samuel stops momentarily to say, "Your teaching was so much better today, Ms. Goff. The lesson was pretty interesting, and you seemed better prepared. Good for you!"

Why do we judge this student's feedback to be more off-putting than the teacher's? Rankism may be the explanation. Rankist attitudes of superiority can appear in a checkout line, at a doctor's appointment, in family interactions, at a parent-teacher conference. According to Fuller, "It is what people who think they're Somebodies do to people they take for Nobodies" (Fuller, 2003).

We hardly need yet one more label for identifying the difficult people or the difficulties with people in our lives. Yet rankism could provide a perspective on behaviors to which we have given little thought.

Notice the ways in which rankism may function between you and students in your classroom, among co-workers during a meeting, between younger and older students in your school, or between teachers and administrative assistants. Is it noticeable? Is there any reason to try to counterbalance the rankism you spot in any of these settings?

Rankism can be an unwelcome catalyst for difficulties in school relationships. We can remind ourselves that we need not feel superior or inferior, dominant or subservient. Shrewd rebalancing of rankist thoughts helps us acknowledge that both structured and unstructured hierarchical positions exist. Yet we need not revere or demean those who hold them.

53 | STUDENTS BEING FRIENDS

Until recently, "friend" was a beloved term. Signifying an affectionate bond, shared memories, and trusted communications, "friend" was an honorable designation, representing a personal alliance that included fondness. Simply "knowing someone" has not traditionally constituted a friendship.

Do we try too hard to force student friendships? Do we label students *our* friends, even though we know better? Do we muddy the roles in schools and mislabel relationships when we try too hard to promulgate connections and bonds?

Reconsider telling students who their friends are. Especially in younger grades, some teachers refer to all classmates as "friends": "Choose a friend to be your partner." "Check with your friends and make a choice." "Are all our friends present?" "My friends, are you all ready to begin our lesson?"

When we use "friend" as a synonym for "classmate," we may be designating a relationship that does not exist. Teacher-orchestrated friendships can be both risky and confusing as students are developing their often fragile social connections

Rethinking the ways we use the term "friends" in our classrooms is worth reflection. Some students merely become confused when a teacher says, "These are your three friends for this activity." Others may become resentful and angry.

The social milieu of schools is both delicate and sturdy. What might be gained if we help students understand the differences between being a friend and being friendly?

How might students benefit from knowing what being a *friend* means and what being *friendly* looks like? Rather than telling students (or anyone else) that they are friends, we can encourage them to be friendly. We can let them see where *their* preferences for friendships take them.

54 | THE AMBIANCE OF SINGING

Singing is a robust act. Songs that energize can invigorate students for a brain break. An entire student body's singing of the national anthem changes the atmosphere and transforms the singers.

"If singing can foster positive human interaction, maybe that is reason enough for us to engage in it" (Bennett & Bartholomew, 1997, p. 3).

Both teachers who are confident with their voices and those who are not can learn the ambiance-changing power of song in their classrooms. Many of us pull back from the idea of singing with our students. We think we don't have a good voice, that we can't sing, that students may laugh at us.

Music educators, however, will tell you that the best way to get better at singing is to *sing*. Notice how your breath and throat adjust with each pitch as you sing melodies. *That is singing*. Those of us who are saddled with the notion that we cannot sing were most likely told that by someone, perhaps even decades ago. It's time to debunk those life-limiting messages!

We can't learn to jog without jogging. We can't learn to sing without singing.

Recordings can help support singers and encourage them to sing along. Ask your music teacher for pointers on how to increase your singing range and confidence. He/she can also recommend some tried-and-true songs that have school-appropriate lyrics.

What kind of music should you sing with your students? Calming and energizing music. Popular music and oldies. Seasonal music and favorite standards. Accompanied and unaccompanied songs. Movie and television themes. Music that prompts dance moves and music that elicits simple gestures. Sing it all.

The ambiance of singing is real. We feel the breath. We feel the connections. We feel absorbed as we join, full-voiced, in singing with our students.

Singing can become a powerful, contributing influence in schools. See if you agree. Be bold. *Sing.*

Singing is infinitely better than yelling. It gives young and old a feeling of security—if not of amusement. Anyone can do it. Everyone should experience what a difference singing makes. (Hifler, 1992, p. 313)

55 | NEUTRAL RESPONSIVENESS

Learning how to offer neutral responses, in schools and elsewhere, can improve the tenor of relationships and the environment for learning. When we "neutral up," we offer comments rather than judgments, observations rather than evaluations.

Neutrally responsive statements can be evidence that we are listening to or participating in an activity or conversation. Yet the neutrality of our responses relieves us from delivering a position or opinion. Communication flows because the emphasis is on interacting and acknowledging, rather than opining and evaluating.

- "I see."
- "I didn't know that."
- "My poor ears!"
- "What an idea!"
- "You're thinking!"
- "You may be on to something."
- "I'm listening."
- "I've heard you say that before."

When we speak with neutral responsiveness, we are neither criticizing nor complimenting; we are neither harsh nor gushy; we are neither agreeable nor disagreeable.

One small caveat about our delivery is important here. Be aware that if we speak with too *little* meaning in our voice, conversational commentary can fall short, feeling too manipulative, too programmed, or too detached.

Neutral responses can sound playful, highly engaged, or mildly interested without being agreeable or disagreeable. Neutrality offers a low-stakes participation in conversations and allows us to be responsive without conveying a position.

As your students are busy learning or your colleagues are busy pondering, try being neutrally responsive as you interact with them. See what happens.

56 | CONVERTING STRESS TO PRESSURE

"I am totally stressed." "This is so stressful." How often do we say these words? What if, each time we announce that we are stressed, we are injecting ourselves with a toxic brew of chemicals?

Stress is a high-profile affliction in this society and is often identified as the cause of various maladies we may contract. Many of us identify what we are feeling as stress simply because that is the easiest and most in-vogue terminology for our condition. The term "stress" has been used to describe bad moods, fatigue, excitement, anxiety, and tensions. But do all those feelings equate with stress? Actually, no.

Real stress is *threat*. Threat creates a primal response in which our body produces the necessary chemicals to enable us to fight or flee. "Threat is what some power, usually a person or group, can do and may very well do to harm us" (Hart, 1983, p. 110).

If we make a distinction between *stress* and *pressure*, perhaps the destructive impacts of stress will become clearer. "Threat is not the same as pressure—one may rush to catch a train or plane with worry and fear about missing it, but without threat" (Hart, 1983, p. 110).

The popularization of the term "stress" has taken a toll on us. Labeling our feelings as stressful can actually make them feel worse. Stress is unhealthy because it eats away at our armor of self-protection and self-determination.

Pressure, on the other hand, can give us momentum to act. Unlike stress, "pressure can be a constructive, propelling force in our reactions to life situations" (Bennett & Bartholomew, 1997, p. 159).

"I'm feeling the pressure to get my reading done." "The pressure to learn this new program is taking a lot more energy than I thought it would." "I'm under a lot of pressure to make a decision." Pressure can be a contributor to resiliency.

Try switching your language use from "stress" to "pressure" and see if that makes a difference in minimizing your image of worry or sense of threat.

57 | PRIVACY FOR US

It is difficult to know the consequences of sharing private information with co-workers. Even when our school friends are eager listeners, curious conversationalists, and supportive responders, it is judicious to think about our personal privacy. Many of us have had to learn a sense of privacy. Some of us do not think much about it.

Ask, "What do I want to keep private about myself in my school?" "Do I monitor the stories and experiences (my own or others') that I share with school staff?" "Do I acknowledge that listeners make assumptions about my life that I may never know have been made?"

Very few confidants will be as careful with our words and our intentions as we are. Our acceptable boundaries for risky behaviors, family habits, and health challenges may not match those of our school colleagues. Be savvy. Appropriately withholding information or diverting the focus in response to a personal question is not rude and may be judicious.

A weekend trip to gamble, a potentially serious health diagnosis, the intent to seek a new job—how do we decide what to keep private? Because our co-workers are our most frequent social group, do we feel free to share all our experiences, in schools and out?

Unbridled openness can be risky for professional comportment and grounded personal behaviors. *Once shared, private information cannot be unshared.* Where do we draw the line for our personal privacy?

Being strategic about privacy in schools is both wise and practical. *We* set our boundaries for the personal information we do and do not share with co-workers. And that line will likely move—indeed, perhaps it needs to be adjusted—with age and experience.

Keeping a secret tends to have a "shelf life," based on the memory, mood, and ethics of the listener. Consider making a distinction between "school talk" and "home talk." When we keep our personal lives private, we have a better chance of deciding what of our lives is and is not shared in schools.

Maintaining personal privacy need not dampen or inhibit strong ties and warm relationships with colleagues. These important privacy decisions let *us* determine the parameters of our communications. When we live our lives with such wisely informed decisions, we feel strong, mature, and self-satisfied.

Confession may be good for the soul, but it seldom makes the one that heard it feel good. The need to clear the air or get something out in the open can cause a bigger rift than the reason for confessing in the first place. (Hifler, 1992, p. 181)

58 | THE WISDOM OF DELAY

In schools, the volume and frequency of questions and decisions can be smothering on some days. With fast-paced inquiries and lickety-split decisions, we may forget the value and necessity of *pausing*.

- "I'll get back to you about that."
- "Let me think about how I want to respond."
- "Tomorrow I'll let you know what the consequences will be."
- "I'll consider your request and let you know of my decision."

Replying immediately is not always a good idea. Whether reacting to a proposal, an infraction, or a critical remark, delaying our reply can be wise.

Of course, there are times when a delay may be inappropriate or ineffective. One way to choose is to take three seconds to decide whether a situation or a person is demanding an immediate response. Then make a judgment about how to offer the best response.

- In response to a co-worker's request to change a schedule or delay a project: "Let me consider what is involved with that change, and I'll let you know shortly."
- A parent notifies you that her child will miss an upcoming, required event: "I'm startled to hear that. I want to consider the implications before I give you my response."
- An administrator expects you to discontinue your beloved annual school program: "This comes as a shock. I want to have a conversation about this, but not right now. I'll make an appointment for tomorrow."

Brief postponement of a response can offer the strength of a deep breath, the perspective of further query, and the potential of a calm, reasoned rejoinder. Whether our delay is twenty-four minutes or twenty-four hours, we take time to craft our response. And we often feel the vivid sense of strength, centeredness, and power that results.

For self-preservation, as well as fair-mindedness and even-handedness toward others, consider the wisdom of delay. Hesitation can have its benefits.

59 | SENSORY THRESHOLDS

Pet peeves about others' behaviors are normal. When a particular behavior occurs daily in a classroom, however, it can drive a teacher (and students) to severe annoyance. The key to minimizing issues is remembering that our frenzy over someone's quirky behavior is more often *our* problem than *theirs*.

Our five senses function to orient us in the world, to give us information about what is happening outside our skin. Visual, auditory, kinesthetic, olfactory, and gustatory senses work constantly to feed us information. When we have a "sensory sensitivity," we can become anxious and intolerant, often reaching our threshold quite quickly.

Kinesthetic: leg jiggling, close proximity, itchy fabrics, touching and hugging, close talking, an uncomfortable chair, pain thresholds (squeezing a hand or shoulder), room temperature

Auditory: gum popping, fingernails on metal or slate, loud throat clearing or chewing, scraping teeth on a fork, screech of tires and birds, loud talking, whispering, alarms and honking, pencil tapping

Visual: messy desk, clashing colors, too much or too little
decor, crooked picture frames, hair too long or too short,
chairs not in alignment, too much light/not enough light

Olfactory: strong smells of raw onions, fish, sweat, old
carpet, perfume

Gustatory: texture and taste of squid, eggs, unbuttered toast

The key to tolerance for our own sensory tipping points is to avoid blaming the offender. We acknowledge that these are *our* sensitivities, not everyone else's. We choose wisely whether or not to reveal our sensitivities. Others often cannot imagine we have such strong aversions to sensations they like or do not even notice. And someone of any age may choose to use our sensitivities to rile us.

Take a deep breath and minimize your response with a bit of private humor: "I'll just move over here to give you a bit more room." "I'm going to pretend I don't hear that sound." "I will *not* threaten to nail his shoe to the floor to stop his leg from jiggling!"

60 | TEACHER AS ENTERTAINER

Some educators become troubled when they watch award ceremonies for teachers and news segments about schools. Very often in those settings, videos show teachers engaged in dramatic, highly animated activity. Nearly all have bold personalities, and students' enthusiasm can verge on frenetic.

Why might educators be troubled about these images of education? Because the implicit message seems to be that full-throttle dramatic behavior equates with teaching. That groups jumping and shouting equates with learning.

Animation can be delivered on a sliding scale that we turn up or turn down, based on students' learning needs and desires. Varying intensities of verbal and nonverbal communication are important for all teachers to master. Vocal expression and volume, posture, eye contact and expression, gestures, movement, and proximity—all are behaviors that contribute to our animation and teaching personae.

If we generate all the energy and excitement in the room, we may be missing out on helping *all* our students learn. If we treat teaching as entertainment, as our performance of the lesson, we may be missing out on learning *how* our students learn.

Variation in intensities and types of animation is pedagogically sound and educationally warranted. Quiet and calm may need infusions of bold and invigorated. Boisterous and loud may need times of peaceful and hushed . . . all for the benefit of student learning.

A self-check may help us reflect on teaching tendencies and ponder the point at which our entertainer personalities may be subduing students' learning.

- Are we the primary generator of ideas during our classes?
- Do we rely on quips, jokes, and teasing to engage students?
- Does our level of animation and drama drive the class and the lesson?
- Does the proportion of our teacher-talk greatly outweigh student-talk?
- Do we value quiet, hesitant student contributions as much as eager, enthusiastic ones?

It is every teacher's challenge to notice and adapt for the benefit of students. Whether our comfort lies in being "a sage on the stage" or "a guide at the side," we know that we likely need to do both for the benefit of students' learning.

6 | VALUING THE VOLLEY

Playing fetch with your dog can be fun . . . but only if your pet returns the ball. As with sports and games, the challenge and unpredictability of the volley (the turn-taking) inspires alertness and lively participation (Bennett, 2012).

The value of "returning tosses" is important for teaching. Lecture mode, the stereotypic "sage on the stage," places nearly all the responsibility on the learner to listen and absorb. In this format, the teacher delivers information rather than involves the students in an exchange of ideas, questions, and interpretations.

When responsibility is placed on students to silently take notes, memorize, and record, many can struggle to learn. When we find ways to engage listening, students can kindle interest and create a volley of ideas. Teachers breathe life into their lessons and their students when they use volley in their teaching.

The same can be said for volley in conversation. Do you know someone whose mode of conversation is talking but not listening? Whose conversational style is more soliloquy than volley? Those folks tend to hold forth rather than exchange ideas. They apparently need a listener rather than a conversation. All of us do at times. They may be desperate to tell rather than ask or compare. With one-sided talkers, a forced interruption may be necessary if we want to make a point.

Being willing to suspend our "talking turn," at least momentarily, in order to include others in the discourse is a sign of maturity, social acumen, and interest in others' points of view.

To initiate a volley, try these options for inserting your voice, for prompting the give-and-take of conversation.

- "I would rather have that expectation modified. Do you want to know why?"
- "Let me describe this to you. Then I'll be eager to know what you think."
- "I know I'm interrupting, but I want our communication to be mutual."

Schools thrive on spirited communications, respectful conversations, and interactive teaching. Valuing the volley of turn-taking in communication is an important skill for all of us. Notice your own sense of volley and the ways it can enliven teaching, learning, and conversation. Practice volleying with others. See what happens.

62 | CULTIVATING CURIOSITY

"I wonder . . ." This simple phrase projects an openness to possibilities. It reveals a readiness to contemplate. It suggests a willingness to explore and be momentarily confused.

When we cultivate curiosity in our classes, we enter into a world of possibility, and we invite our students to join us:

- "What would happen if . . . ?"
- "How could we solve this problem?"
- "What might be a reason that happened?"
- "Can you imagine why he said that? What might he have meant?"
- "How would you explain her idea?"

Whether in the classroom or in the teachers' lounge, showing interest in another's ideas can prompt mutual wondering. Being curious about what and how others think can be a purposeful attitude. Curiosity invites questions: "How did you figure that out?" "What made you decide on that choice?"

When we release ourselves from the "one answer" orientation that standardized testing can produce, we spark vibrancy in our students. Creative problem-solving can become a habit of mind, a natural way to think. Whether the problem is tangible or imagined, opening students' minds to "What else could it be?" can enliven their interest in learning and their fascination with their own minds.

Whether in the context of a lesson, a creative project, or a conflict resolution, cultivating curiosity can open us to questions we may never have asked and understandings we may never have imagined.

63 | ASPIRE TO EXCEL

On some days teachers need to just "get by." It's self-preservation. But when we let this minimalist effort become our habit, we are giving up on our dreams.

We didn't become teachers just to get a job. We became teachers to shape young minds, to make the world a better place, to offer support and guidance to young people, to share our passion for learning, to bring life to our classes and our students. We aspire to *educate*. A teacher who "aspires to excel is almost by default a visionary . . . a leader" (Raessler, 2003, p. 5).

Schools can breed challenges and spirit-breaking experiences. Yet becoming dispirited about mandates, regulations, procedures, testing, and standards is no reason to give up on our dreams for students. If anything, those are the times to buckle down and work harder.

Bolster determination. Ignite students' interest. Ballast emotions with resolve to be our best and do our best. These are the aspirations that revitalize us. When we aspire to excel we can reconfigure our attitudes and behaviors. We can aim to bring out the best in ourselves and others.

Nine Ways to Excel in Schools

1. *Start the day with intention.* Be clear and simple about your resolve.
2. *Hold on to the best of you.* Use that as a starting point to recover your aspirations.
3. *Ignite your energy in the classroom.* Stimulate engagement and interactions.
4. *Subdue your energy in the classroom.* Stimulate quietness. Let students take the lead.
5. *Prompt learning.* Use unique, clever, and challenging ways to hook students' interest.
6. *Show yourself.* Let others see your interest and verve for learning.
7. *Shift your classroom persona.* Be the teacher you most admire.
8. *Treat your students the way you would want your own children to be treated.* Show respect, curiosity, compassion, and loving expectation.
9. *Read, study, and query others.* Find best practices to energize your classroom.

64 | SOMEONE LOVES THEM

- A friendship goes sour, and you can hardly tolerate someone who was once a close friend.
- A colleague who once rankled you becomes your most ardent supporter.
- A beloved relative did the unthinkable, and you furiously sever all ties.

Whether it is love or hate, we tend to be "all in" with our strong emotions. We operate under the 100 percent rule, believing someone is totally terrible or totally wonderful. *Yet the rule is not really a rule at all; it's a fallacy.* It misleads us.

Citizens from countries once at war become friends. Beloved associates fall from grace and become nemeses. Swings in friendship can cause us to adore or detest wholeheartedly. Reality, however, provides the wisdom to question whether someone is *ever* totally unlovable or unhateable. When we see the 100 percent rule for what it is, a narrow view through a narrow lens, we can step back and consider a more balanced perspective. We can take another view of others and ourselves.

Many different thinkers have told us that "what we resist, persists." The more we resist some*thing* or some*one*, the more we strengthen that thing's or person's effect on us. We detest a co-worker; that emotion ties us to her. We believe the secretary snubs us; we begin spotting her other faults. *We look for behaviors to confirm our opinions*. And we are so certain of our opinions that we often find that evidence, *whether or not it exists*.

Letting go of our animosity frees us from negative thoughts and behaviors that can deplete our emotional health. We see our foe as unlikable, unlovable. Yet someone likes him. Someone loves her. *Someone genuinely loves that person.*

Severely negative portraits we hold of others can fester like an abscess on our psyche. Are we willing to release someone from the 100 percent rule? Are we willing to reframe our perceptions? Imagine how it would feel to rid yourself of that infection. When we use our power to soften assumptions and broaden images, we contribute to our own good health. We release others' hold on us. And we know *someone loves them*.

> We all know difficult people. I have only to glimpse such a person from afar, and immediately everything about her repels me: the slant of her mouth, the shrug of her shoulders, the tone of her voice, the cut of her dress. Although she has a husband, children, and friends, it's inconceivable to me that they could love such a woman. The power of my antipathy freezes her inside an image that seems fixed for eternity . . . . Then I recall how just a few months ago, merely to think of her would bring a warm smile to my face.

What changed? The trouble might have started with nothing more than a careless barbed remark or an insensitive comment that opened up an old wound. As that hurt began to fester, steadily fueled by new suspicions and resurrected grievances, my perception of her shifted. (Batchelor, 2004)

65 | PROBLEM-SOLVING

Teachers are expert problem-solvers. Whether it is figuring out how to get shoelaces untangled or how to solve a thorny algebraic equation, teachers are industrious.

Does anyone *teach* us how to solve problems? Maybe not. Our daily experiences and our diligent efforts to "figure it out" seem to be the most potent problem-solving skill builders.

For some of us, problems make us eager; we treat problem-solving as a mystery, almost a game. Others approach problems like obstacles, deterrents to efficiency in learning and teaching. Asking for help can be one solution. Yet, as Curwin and Mendler advise in their seminal work describing discipline with dignity, be savvy about whom you ask for help: "Along with calming ourselves when angry, we need to be good at figuring out how to solve problems we have or that others try to give us. If we let other people give us their solutions, then they have power over us . . . . Each of us has the power to make our own decisions, and we need to decide who we will allow to influence us and who we won't" (Curwin & Mendler, 1997, p. 94).

The two authors also provide a succinct, six-step solution for problem-solving. The clear, practical advice may help those who struggle with this issue, at whatever age, in whatever setting.

Techniques for Solving Problems: The Six-Step Solution

1. *Stop and calm down.* Pay attention to the signs that your body gives you when it feels tense.
2. *Think.* Consider your options. Think about the many different actions you can choose to take.
3. *Decide.* Choose a goal: what do you want to happen? Think about the consequences: what will happen if you actually do what you are thinking?
4. *Choose a second solution, in case the first solution doesn't work.* Always have a backup plan ready.
5. *Act.* Carry out your decision.
6. *Evaluate.* Did you reach your goal? If the same problem occurs again, what will you do? Are there any people (parents, friends, teachers) who might help you as you figure out the best solution? (Curwin and Mendler, 1997, p. 99)

66 | ALLOWING UPSET

Teachers fix things. We face a myriad of fixings daily. We unscramble misunderstandings, clarify errors, and soothe hurt feelings. We don't always get it right, but we so often try.

Our compassion and love for students seep into our responses to them. We want them to be happy, comfortable, and at ease. But sometimes we witness their *dis*-ease. They are angry, hurt, disappointed. They pout. All these reactions are normal parts of growing and living. But what do we *do* about them? How do we make it better? How can we *fix* the upset?

We know we can be compassionate about students' feelings. Yet sometimes it is the "letting go of fixing" that can challenge us. Can we be strong enough to allow others to be upset? Can we let anger, disappointment, or frustration run its course rather than try to alleviate it? Can we know whether it is time to intervene or let it be?

When others are out of sorts, we sometimes need to allow them simply to experience it. Important growth develops for us all when we realize, "I'll be okay. I'm just going to be angry [hurt, disappointed] for a while."

Allowing others to be upset is not the same as ignoring their troubles. Compassion and assistance are perennial foundations of being a teacher. We can be kind as we allow others to be upset. They can feel the bad feelings and live through them. They can learn that their hurt is temporary. They can learn that they will bounce back, and when they do, we'll be right there to help them move along.

67 | I COULD BE WRONG

"I could be wrong." How comfortable are you with making that statement?

Sometimes we teachers develop a fear of being wrong. We may need to be right, to let others know when they are right, and to avoid or hide from being wrong. Other than with factual material, what is wrong with being wrong? Could we benefit, even a little, from exploring comfort with "I could be wrong"? Would it help us?

Our interactions and self-assurance often change when we adopt a no-fear orientation toward wrongness. As uncomfortable as it may be initially, making peace with "I could be wrong" can have far-reaching benefits.

- We settle into comfort with a variety of possible right answers.
- We let go of our "fear of wrong" and stay open to additional interpretations.
- We release our need to argue an opposing view; we let it pass by.
- We shed the stress that comes with defending our rightness.
- We free ourselves from minutiae that ultimately do not matter.

- We help our students release distress associated with fear of wrongness.
- We feel no competition to win our version of "rightness."

When there is no competition to be right, we can let go of the struggle. We are not worried or fretful, because our inquisitive orientation leads us to resolution. Our fear morphs into curiosity about others' perspectives. *We regain our vitality. We regain our courage.*

Rejecting opinions is not a requirement, because we are open to plural possibilities. We let potential mini-competitions dissolve. *We regain our sense of goodwill.*

Living "I could be wrong" can alleviate tension. We shed the dichotomy that "right" is strength and "wrong" is weakness. We no longer defend stances that may not matter. We open ourselves to curiosity about others' opinions and recollections.

68 | TAKING YOUR BEST SELF TO SCHOOL

So many expectations feel like they are consuming us. Lesson planning, committee work, test preparation, learning new material . . . and on and on. The stress caused by living in constant anxiety can interfere with sleep, mood, digestion, resilience, and, of course, good teaching (Bennett & Suarez, 2016, p. 14).

Too easily and too frequently, we can find ourselves in perpetual fight-or-flight mode, readying ourselves for battle or to run and hide.

When we consciously choose the intention to be our best, all sorts of interactions, big and small, shift our focus and recast our feelings. Manifesting our intent each morning can powerfully frame the way we want to behave, react, comment, and care.

- *Breathe in* the attitude and behaviors you want to feel and portray.
- *Exhale* the tension, doubt, and fear that subdue your joy.
- *Set a tone* for relationships by warmly greeting those in school.
- *Show your concern* by listening to those who are troubled.

- *Spread goodwill* by words and deeds that support others.
- *Acknowledge and affirm* if you cannot support.
- *Grasp* every opportunity to be the best teacher you can be.

The simple yet powerful attitudes and behaviors described here will not take away the hard, sometimes tedious work that is required of all educators. The challenges are givens. We know the work is difficult, *and we do it anyway*.

Regaining the life in our teaching may require us to take baby steps as we experiment with what works for us. Our mental, physical, and social health is worth every step.

69 | DEFINING TRUST

Imagine yourself saying, "I just don't trust him." It's not an uncommon thing to say. But what conclusions do your listeners draw when they hear that?

"I just don't trust her" can set off all sorts of alarms, all sorts of conjectures. But what does that statement really mean? Is she likely to tell lies, miss deadlines, cheat on report cards? Do you believe she changes her mind frequently, is too friendly, arrives late to school? Not all accusations of "untrustworthiness" are equally dire.

Are we willing to become quizzical about an "I don't trust him" statement? By asking the clarifying question "You don't trust him to do what?" we can illuminate the meaning. And the accusation of being untrustworthy is almost always worth a closer look.

"I don't trust him to get his work done" addresses a type of trust very different from that associated with "I don't trust him to deposit all the donated money." In the same way, "I don't trust her understanding of the curriculum" involves a different notion of trust than "I don't trust her to report accurate scores."

Trust is an attribute that is very precious to most of us. We would likely be hurt and worried if we knew that someone had stated he didn't trust us. And in the close communities of schools, a statement of distrust can usurp goodwill and collegiality.

The next time we hear the statement "I don't trust him," we could ask, "What has caused you to lose that trust?" Clarifying the accusation could give everyone relief and perspective, including the speaker. When these moments of relief and clarity settle into the fabric of our schools, we can feel the revival of energy, vitality, and momentum.

70 | JUMPING TO CONCLUSIONS

He walks down the hall toward you. You are the only two in the hallway. You look at him, ready to smile and offer a cheery "Good morning!" With eyes downcast, he walks by you as if you are not there. What is your reaction?

- *Indignation.* "Who does he think he is, not bothering to even look at me?"
- *Irritation.* "Why can't he make the effort to say a simple hello?"
- *Superiority.* "With such poor social skills, he shouldn't even be a teacher."
- *Meanness.* Silently you smirk at his indifference, eager to tell co-workers about this perceived slight.
- *Affirmation.* "I knew he didn't like me, and since no one is around, he doesn't even pretend!"
- *Anger.* "How dare he act so superior!"

It may be a challenge to interpret this scene as anything but snobbery or poor manners. Yet the same curiosity and compassion that help us determine what our students need in order to learn can serve us well with other adults.

The *illusion* in this scenario is our belief that we know the reason for another's behaviors. The *pitfall* of this conclusion is the missed opportunity to wonder with good intentions. The *risk* to professional relationships is the narrow labeling of another's behaviors and personalizing their intent.

Asking ourselves "What else could it be?" implies that we have the power and presence of mind to press the pause button to offer a broader palette of possibilities.

- Is he preoccupied with an upcoming meeting?
- Is he concerned about a loved one?
- Is he mentally preparing for his first class?
- Is he an introvert who is much more comfortable keeping to himself than offering easy banter or automatic greetings?

Why not be your best by offering a warm greeting to him *with no expectation for receiving one in return*?

When faced with puzzling behaviors, we can avoid jumping to conclusions. We can take a moment, have a second thought. This opening of possibility offers a moment of grace to ourselves and our co-workers. We choose to suspend judgment for the good of the moment and for nourishing goodwill in schools.

71 | RESILIENCE

Troubles are inevitable and necessary in schools. Yet when we are in the midst of them, we can feel hopeless and chronically agitated. Key here is our *resilience*: how quickly and easily do we bounce back from turmoil?

A basketball can provide a rich metaphor for bouncing back. Compression is key to a basketball functioning properly. An underinflated basketball has little resilience, does not bounce well, and may not behave or look like a basketball. The same is true for teachers.

Very likely we will get sick, have our feelings hurt, not measure up to expectations. *Very likely.* So the key is not to dodge these silent missiles that come our way. The key is to learn how to be resilient, to bounce back, to regain our composure.

Like a basketball, those within schools can expect to have times of inflation and deflation. A total absence of conflict and disagreement is not an option. Both are natural and necessary.

Do you know what deflates or causes you to be underinflated? Fatigue, conflict, discord, confusion, loss of trust, fear, disincentive, sense of failure.

Do you know what inflates you, what restores your compression? Nutrition, hydration, exercise, conversation with a friend, inspiring ideas, change of routine, listening to music, laughing, feeling powerful and vibrant.

Adversity is not what depletes us. Absence of resilience does.

If we were able to view major or minor difficulties as natural, normal, and valuable events, would our responses to them change? Would we be able to accept rather than resent them?

Being hostile toward any of life's difficulties only amplifies our discomfort, and we end up at war with ourselves, arguing with our lives rather than living them. (Carroll, 2006, p. 6)

72 | BEWARE OF EXPERTS

Some of us believe that experts know better than we do. And some of us believe "it ain't necessarily so."

Ideally, we all have expertise with our subjects. We have studied long and hard, and we continue to pursue professional development opportunities, wanting to get better and know more. Likewise, in the context of classrooms, we know our students better than nearly anyone. It is important to embrace the knowledge that *we are the experts* in our classrooms with our own students.

Often, professionals attain the designation of expert through wide and varied exposure: publications, presentations, and educational materials. All these avenues of visibility are impressive accomplishments and show dedication to the topic. Then why would we need to *beware* of experts?

Experts, even self-appointed ones, tend to hold tightly to the ideas that earned them their stature. But that devotion to ideas can come at the expense of flexibility, necessary modification, and appropriate adaptability. What do we do when expert recommendations do not match our knowledge of the needs of our students and schools? This can be a gnarly dilemma for sure.

The vitality and wisdom of our own understandings can be tamped down when we are told to substitute expert opinion for our own. And what do we do when experts change their minds? How are teachers informed of the new adaptations *or* the faulty logic of the required program?

Good ideas can go awry. Good ideas are rarely a panacea. Caution about wholeheartedly adopting expert recommendations is based in the reality that *we* are the ones most knowledgeable about our classrooms, schools, and communities.

When we pair informed caution with fervent searches for best practices, we place expert opinion where it belongs. We vigorously pursue the best for our students, whether that best comes from us or expert opinion.

Seek expert opinion. Watch for wisdom. Weigh the viability for *your* students, in *your* classes, at *your* school.

Self-determination implies that we have choice-making skills that allow us to consider similar and disparate points of view and that we assume responsibility for the choices we are making. (Bennett & Bartholomew, 1997, p. 186)

73 | RESPONSIVE PROFESSIONALISM

"Professionalism." A definition of this important term and concept for comportment in schools can be a bit elusive. Yet some of us spend our careers aiming to achieve and sustain the qualities that make us professional.

Professionalism suggests the expectation of being an informed, competent, proficient, and knowledgeable teacher. For some, professionalism also means a standard of attire or appearance. Sensitivity toward off-limits topics and potentially volatile issues in schools can be another aspect of the honorific "She is very professional!"

Being a *responsive* professional may be a bit more specific. For schools to be their most efficient and cooperative, we educators pay attention to our standard of professionalism. We sustain a conscience *and* a conscientiousness about *all* facets of the school community.

In addition to general commitments such as ethical treatment and behaviors, some more subtle choices can set the standard for professional conduct.

- *Do we reply to communications and deadlines in a timely and thorough manner?* Emails, texts, and requests from school personnel deserve a prompt reply, *even when we think they don't.* If the response must be delayed, write a reply stating that, and let the sender know when to expect the response. We can cause distress and frustration when we do not respect the timelines others need to make. Sometimes we compromise *their* responsibilities to others when we delay ours.

- *Do we prepare our written work with meticulous attention to accuracy and appearance?* The work we produce—reports, proposals, emails, notes to parents, and so on—is a signature statement of our professionalism. Proofread for accuracy and clarity.

- *Do we take a very cautious approach to participating in non-school-related activities during school hours?* Taking and making private calls, sending personal messages, running errands, interacting on social media, or doing personal business during school hours may be considered mismanagement of time at best, and a breach of ethics at worst. Be savvy about what you do and do not do with your time at school.

Schools and teaching ask the best of us. Students and parents deserve the best of us. Pursue high expectations. Savor the expertise you embody when you practice responsive professionalism.

74 | TEACHER FRIENDSHIPS

If we had the choice, some of us would wish our school community could be a happy group of dear friends. We would support and compliment each other daily. We would host dinners in our homes. We would celebrate weekly happy hours. We would feel that our faculty and staff were more like a social club than professional acquaintances.

Yet is it possible for us *all* to be friends? Is that even desirable? The expectation that social compatibilities and friendships are unanimous in schools is rarely a reality and almost never sustained. So how do we adopt reasonable expectations for the waxing and waning of friendships in schools? We rethink our expectations about friends.

Some friends are movie friends. Some are travel friends. Some are confidants. Some were in our lives long ago, and those memories are what sustains our friendship. With some, we almost exclusively share stories of raising children. With others, our friendship is based on being neighbors. Hobbies, exercising, and organizations all can bring us in touch with budding friendships in schools.

In life, our friends can vary in their levels of enthusiasm, senses of adventure, priorities for advancement, and knowledge of our work. If we expect the same criteria for all friendships, we are likely limiting the quality of our own life experiences. Our "best friend" may not be our best friend in all ways or for all times. And we may even have several best friends.

The values of kind, appreciative, and respectful school relationships are priceless. And the vitality and ambiance of our schools depend on them. Can we contribute to that ambiance by pondering the parameters of school friendship both among students and among teachers?

Rethinking the designation of "friend" can help us sort out the identities and expectations we have for friends in schools. Embrace the varying depths and characteristics of friendships. Richness resides there.

75 | COMPASSION AND HAPPINESS

Teachers are among the most compassionate people on the planet. The foundation of our work is *caring*. We care about people: who they are as students and who they will be as adults.

Compassion is "a mental attitude based on the wish for others to be free of their suffering" (Dalai Lama & Cutler, 1998, p. 114). Compassion compels us to act, but it does not necessarily come easily to all of us. Caring can seem arduous; it can take effort to monitor and revise our reactions to others.

Few other professions have workers who feel and display such compassionate attention to so many, every day, over the course of their careers. Some of us enter the profession with boundless compassion; others of us have to learn compassion as situations arise that call for us to show it.

And given the amount of tragedy and suffering we are exposed to, how can we muster the ability to show compassion? When difficulties threaten, many of us want to bear down, sharpen our defenses, and toughen our resistance.

"No matter how much violence or how many bad things we have to go through, I believe that the ultimate solution to our conflicts, both internal and external, lies in returning to our basic

or underlying human nature, which is gentle and compassionate" (Dalai Lama & Cutler, 1998, 56).

The Dalai Lama believes that compassion is the key to happiness. Demonstrating our compassion for others can be an
antidote to the separateness we sometimes feel. In small, quiet
ways, we can show compassion and contribute to a school-wide
sense of kinship and affinity.

76 | CONTAGION OF BEHAVIOR

Like a cold, the flu, and other communicable diseases, poor behavior can be contagious in schools. So can good behavior.

We all know students who, just by their presence, seem to have an effect on the entire class. Some stir up the environment, always a bit goading, laughing, sulking. Others keep things calm; they are eager to do their work, encouraging others, setting a tone for quiet achievement. Each affects the classroom "stew."

Teachers can be catalysts for other teachers' achievements, large and small. We can set the standard for helpful, supportive behavior. In small but potent ways, we can spread goodwill. We can acknowledge others' efforts. We can make things better. We can spread wellness.

- *To teachers struggling with challenges:* "That's a very difficult issue to deal with. Let me know how I can help."
- *To teachers who are calm and caring:* "You are so consistently caring, even when you need to issue a punishment. I appreciate having that model."

- *To teachers who produce quality work:* "Everything you create shows quality in content and appearance. I notice these things."

Our contagion of behavior can also productively influence non-teaching personnel in schools: "The way you manage all these hidden facets of our school helps us all. Thank you."

We sometimes expect administrators to give compliments, but we may not expect to give them to administrators ourselves: "What a lot you juggle behind the scenes every single day. Thank you for all you do to make our school run smoothly."

In whatever ways and with whatever words we offer them, our supportive comments can make a world of difference to the health of our schools. Our contagion of goodwill can offer moments of vitality to all who receive it.

77 | AIM FOR UNDERSTANDING

When someone agrees with us, we can feel validated and relieved. When someone disagrees, we can bristle at the implication that we are wrong. Some of us develop a habit of looking for agreement. Some of us have little tolerance for being wrong.

During conflict, we can hold tightly to our positions, building a case for why we believe what we believe. We may know those who feel an innate preparation for combat when they sense disagreement. More treacherous than the disagreement itself can be the backstories we tell ourselves about reasons for the conflict. We make assumptions. We assume we know the intent of another's choices.

How can we momentarily suspend our assumptions and shift our focus to a path toward understanding? Key here is communication. Asking questions in order to understand, rather than arguing to convince, widens our prospects for resolution (Rusk, 1993).

With a calm demeanor and conversational tone, we open ourselves to listening and problem-solving. Simple questions and statements, spoken with calm curiosity, not sarcasm or aggression, can pave the path to understanding.

- "What happened that made you think that?"
- "Can you tell me a little more about what led you to that decision?"
- "Interesting. I had a very different reaction. Tell me how you interpreted that."
- "What can you tell me that will help me understand what just happened?"

If the other person happens to explain his or her opinion without asking yours, simply say, "Now I better understand your position. Let me tell you my thoughts, so you can understand my perspective as well."

Agreement is not always necessary for peaceful solutions. We need not feel threatened by conflicting views or actions. Responding to conflict by aiming to understand rather than agree (Rusk, 1993) can release the pressure valve of resistance, refuel each party's vitality, and reenliven our presence in schools.

78 | PERSEVERE

Being a teacher can be hard.

- We invest ourselves wholeheartedly, yet sometimes our efforts fall short.
- We know our subject matter, but students may seem uninterested.
- We search for more and better ways to teach, but the results can be disappointing.

As educators, we will fail. We will be hurt. We will be disappointed. We will be discouraged. Yet key to our recovery from these slumps is what we *tell* ourselves about those failures.

What do we need to do? "Just get up."

"Just get up!" With this statement, Olympic gold medal figure skater Scott Hamilton reminds us that the challenges of a skater involve many falls and frequent pain. It is *impossible* to be a skater and not fall down. *All* skaters fall. All skaters *fail*. They know they will fall. They know they will fail. They know both will hurt. Hamilton says: "Just get up!"

Too many "falls" without strategies to recover can cause teachers to "crust up." We generate layers of crust to protect us as we cling to our anger, refuse assistance, and numb our bodies, minds, and spirits. But crusting insulates us from feeling and caring, so we miss out on the vitality of our lives. Then "we forget to be glad for all the things that go right" (Hifler, 1992, p. 327).

When we know how to "get up," when we accept that the fall will come again, we can persevere. We feel the strength of our knowing, and we use determination to pull ourselves out of the doldrums. Just get up. Just keep going. Just aspire to do better.

79 | PRINCIPLES OF TEACHING AND LEARNING

A set of principles for teaching and learning can serve us well. We may become more aware of our aims, more consistent in our communications with students and parents, more articulate at stating our positions, more adept at describing our rationales.

There is a security that comes with knowing the principles, the tenets, to which we ascribe. Principles give us a platform for making choices and taking directions. Instead of rudderless improvisation, we can check ourselves to judge if we are on or off the path we have chosen.

"Principles are important to us because they shape boundaries and supply tracks for our choices and behaviors as teachers . . . . Our principles form the foundation on which we base our actions and build our teaching identities . . . . Knowing our principles makes us better teachers. Because we know on what foundations our behaviors are based, we see congruency with those foundations in all that we do, say, and think as we work with students" (Bennett & Bartholomew, 1997, pp. 29–30).

Bennett and Bartholomew's principles for teaching and learning provide one example of principles that can guide our school practices.

Principle 1: Students have the right to be treated with respect and dignity for their ideas, skills, and stages of development.

Principle 2: Students deserve an engaging learning environment in which they feel safe enough to demonstrate freely their understandings and skills through various types of participation.

Principle 3: Student learning is the responsibility of both teachers and students.

Principle 4: Learning is holistic and constructive.

Principle 5: A teacher's attitudes, behaviors, and methodologies should be compatible with one another.

Principle 6: Quality of life is enriched through music and singing. (Bennett & Bartholomew 1997, 32)

80 | INTROVERTS AND EXTROVERTS

Slotting anyone into a one-word category to describe and define that person can feel appalling. Yet it is done. In schools and elsewhere, we categorize in order to inform, to assess, to improve.

The labels "introvert" and "extrovert" have long been used to describe personalities, even though many additional frameworks exist. Considering the two personality categories of "introvert" and "extrovert" in schools can help us better understand our own reactions to their differences. The characteristics may sound familiar to us. We may stereotypically use the labels to identify ourselves and others. Even though these dichotomous personality behaviors can be situational and can alter with age, thinking about them can help us understand our reactions to them.

Some teachers are confident *extroverts* who sweep into a room and immediately receive or command attention. Some of us like to be near extroverts to soak up their energy and humor, their attention and charm. Extroverts have been described as "people magnets" who draw everyone to them, even though not all extrovert demeanors are pleasant.

Although it may be tempting, we should not assume that those with quiet personalities wish they could be more like the exuberant ones. Extroverts may get their social sustenance from others. But some of us shy away from the dramatic energy and the big presence extroverts may exude. The personality can feel like too much energy. It can feel exhausting.

A confident *introvert* may quietly step into a room and neither need nor desire a fanfare of attention. Introverts appear comfortable being quiet, being observers, being still. We may like to be near introverts to feel a sense of calm, a comfortable stillness. Yet some of us are discomforted by such subdued participation and interaction.

Some may distrust or shy away from introverts' silence, because we may not be able to interpret their mood or gauge their opinions. Because introverts may *appear* to be withdrawn, they can be misjudged as distant, disinterested, uncaring. Their energy may feel restrained and restraining. It can feel exhausting.

Recent literature on extroverts and introverts may explain a widening gulf between the two in American society. In recent decades, bombastic, showy, and bold behaviors have become very prevalent and widely accepted. The now popular entertainer personality, according to cultural historian Warren Susman, contributed to a shift from "a culture of character to a culture of personality" (Cain, 2012, p. 21).

So it is possible that extrovert behavior has become the norm for many in our schools, perhaps for numerous reasons. And it may also be possible that this extreme difference between the two profiles warrants compassionate consideration for both.

As teachers, we have a vital obligation to understand our openness and manage our reactions to *all* personalities, whether bold or quiet, brash or meek. Sometimes such intentions require a momentary setting aside of our preferences and judgments in order to communicate, accept, and teach. We are very capable of that.

81 | A PRACTICE OF PLAYFULNESS

Even when we are not playing, our playful attitudes and behaviors can be a boon to learning and an antidote to discouragement.

Appropriate lighthearted interactions in schools can be "mood vitamins" that serve both the senders and receivers.

- *The faux scold.* Students noisily shove and run to the shelves to get their books. "That wasn't *quite* what I had in mind when I said 'Grab your books.' "
- *Permission to exude.* Students follow the lead of a giggler with loud, enthusiastic laughing. "Okay, this noise level is hurting my ears. Take five seconds to get the giggles out so we can continue."
- *The subtle cease.* Teachers angrily and endlessly complain about a thorny district issue that may prompt a teacher strike. "Okay, this lunchroom talk is disturbing my digestion."
- *The disposition shift.* Teachers begin sniping over their pedagogical differences. "Aren't these students fortunate to have such an *array* of teachers as us!" (Bennett & Suarez, 2016, p. 13)

A "practice of playfulness" has us being lighthearted, sometimes slightly self-effacing, ready to smile with easy humor, but not at another's expense. We offer quippy comments that are momentary connections with friends and strangers. When we notice the charm in others' behaviors, we can infuse our interactions with easygoing banter.

Important here is to stress what playfulness is *not*. It is not the teacher telling jokes, entertaining, dominating the lesson, or being sarcastic.

Instead, playfulness is eagerness to teach with curiosity, engagement, and repartee. If playfulness becomes too clever, too dramatic, or too distracting, students' rowdiness may escalate rather than engage.

See what happens with an occasional scattering of playfulness throughout your day. Adopting this practice in life, even in the midst of harshness or impatience, can revitalize mood, attitude, energy, and ultimately healthy communication for us *and* for those around us.

A master in the art of living draws no sharp distinction between his work and his play, his labour and his leisure, his mind and his body, his education and his recreation. He hardly knows which is which. He simply pursues his vision of excellence through whatever he is doing, and leaves others to determine whether he is working or playing. To himself he always appears to be doing both. (Jacks, 1932, p. 1)

The opposite of play is not work—the opposite of play is depression. (Sutton-Smith, 1998)

Play is as important to humans as vitamins and sleep. (Brown, 2009)

82 | COMPETITION IN THE CLASSROOM

Sometimes the best way to generate eagerness and involvement is to create competition. Whether it is high-stakes or playful, pitting students against one another in pedagogical settings can be fun. It can also be risky.

At times, competition in classrooms can take a toll on learning and create more bad feelings than good. Competition may send unintended messages of superiority and inferiority to the winners and the losers. Competition may ratchet up the energy so that eagerness turns into melee and long-term educational goals are forfeited for short-term classroom engagement.

When participation is expected in classroom competitions, students likely do not have the choice to opt out. Some already know they will fail in front of their peers. Some choose to be goofy or intentionally wrong rather than show their peers how "smart" or "dumb" they are. Some cannot perform under pressure: noise and frantic energy block their ability to think on the spot.

Our whole lives can become a competition when we habitually judge who is better or worse than we are. In classroom contests, incentives like trinkets, privileges, or bragging rights raise the ante.

The "three Be's" can provide some guidance for monitoring the influence of competition in the classroom:

- *Be wise* about the effects of competition for academic purposes.
- *Be savvy* about which students may be less able to access their knowledge during confrontational recall.
- *Be thoughtful* about whether competition is contributing to or detracting from educational goals and achievements.

> We are all competitive by nature, and such impulse can help people achieve things they would never accomplish otherwise . . . . Appeal sparingly to the competitive urge . . . because competition has only limited usefulness. (McGinnis, 1985, p. 128)

83 | ANNOYANCE ANOMALY

HE: Where can I find a pencil?

SHE: In the drawer beside the fridge.

HE [RETURNING]: Where did you say the pencil is?

SHE [STOPPING HER WORK, ENUNCIATING EACH WORD]: I *said* it's in the drawer beside the fridge.

HE [RETURNING ONCE MORE]: What color is it?

SHE [CLEARLY IMPATIENT]: I *don't know*. Yellow? It's the only pencil in the drawer!

HE [RETURNING YET AGAIN]: I can't find it.

With whom do you most sympathize? As the female speaker, could you hear your voice getting increasingly impatient, ready to say something cruel? Can you envision the annoyance in your face, voice, posture, and gritted teeth? As the male speaker, could you feel the innocence of your requests, the honest confusion, the genuine need for help?

This scene taught an important, life-changing lesson to the female speaker. She was desperately trying to meet an important work deadline and was exceedingly annoyed by the continued interruptions. He didn't know that; he just wanted a pencil. He was feeling less sure of himself and more confused with each effort to find the pencil. Does one of them warrant more sympathy than another?

The background to this story was that the male speaker was recovering from a traumatic brain injury. He had no choice other than to behave the way he was behaving. Would that knowledge have changed your reaction if you were the female speaker? Would you have felt differently? Responded differently?

Here was the lesson for the female speaker: Our feeling of annoyance does not mean others are *being annoying*. Likewise, our feeling of anger does not mean others are "making" us angry. Our feeling of being insulted does not mean someone is sending us the insults.

Why not? Because others are just being *them*. We are the ones who *permit* ourselves to interpret and accept the emotions we are feeling. We tacitly agree to feel them.

Initially, there is little connection between *their* behavior and *our* reaction. When we name and consequently *feel* another's action as an offense, we, in essence, glue it to us. It becomes *our* reaction.

When we voluntarily accept offense, we give the other permission to annoy, anger, or insult us. Why do that?

We all know people with annoying habits and behaviors. We acknowledge that they push our buttons. But it is not likely that they push *everyone's* buttons. Some sane, rational, and cognizant people see no problem with the behaviors that bug us. The more we allow and accept being bugged by others, the more our vitality is diminished and tamped down. It is up to us to mitigate our own annoyance, rally for our own vibrancy.

We have the power to develop immunity to the words that sound insulting, the behaviors that feel rude, or the actions that annoy. Simply don't take it in. Dispel and dissipate. Leave it with them. As Eleanor Roosevelt said, "No one can make you feel inferior without your consent."

84 | BEING A BENEFICENT OBSERVER

Beneficent observers reframe others' behaviors to become more open to a range of possible meanings. Instead of assuming rudeness, we consider that the other person has a harried schedule. Instead of assuming coldness, we consider that the other person is painfully shy. Instead of assuming insult, we consider that the other person has no idea this is a sensitive topic for us. Instead of assuming disrespect, we consider that the other person knows little about our classroom expertise and achievements. We choose to think "What else could it be?" rather than assuming a deliberate affront.

When we are beneficent in the ways we see others, we change how we feel about and speak to them *and* the ways we speak to others about them:

1. We contribute to our own sense of calm and stability, our own good health.
2. We feel less like an adversary and more like a strong, compassionate, generous-of-spirit member of the school community.

3. We let them be *them* without taking on the negative views we have of them or that they have of us.

4. We essentially demagnetize ourselves. We are no longer pulled into others' drama. We leave their anger, jealousy, and rude behaviors with them.

5. We realize that *our* own thresholds for tolerance and preferred behaviors may be causing our suffering more than any intentional action by the "offending" person.

6. We are willing to give the other a moment of grace and the benefit of the doubt to see behavior as simply that: behavior (Bennett & Bartholomew, 1997, p. 210).

7. We devote ourselves to helping rather than hindering goodwill.

8. We ask ourselves: "What could I say, do, and think that models compassion?"

9. We sometimes offer a silent benediction to those who rankle us: "May you be well, may you be happy, may you be free from suffering."

These habits of mind happen neither quickly nor easily, but they are worth the effort, inch by inch, step by step, healthy habit by healthy habit.

85 | GUMPTION, GRIT, AND GAIETY

The alliteration is appealing, and so are the images. What would happen if we took gumption, grit, and gaiety to school with us each day?

Gumption is courage to act using common sense. We have a get-up-and-go attitude. We display a spirited initiative to get things done. We have drive and heart.

- We may speak up calmly to disagree with a co-worker.
- We may let a custodian know that we need a change in our room setup and cleaning schedule.
- We may ask the principal to explain a statement made in our annual evaluation.

Grit is tenacity that borders on stubbornness. We see a challenge, we take it on, and we endure. With our firmness of character, challenging situations fuel us. We are persistent.

- We are determined help a student achieve a challenge that baffles him.

- We persevere past our threshold of fatigue and a myriad of obstacles to manage and polish the annual program for parents.
- We know our weaknesses, and we are willing to do what is necessary to develop and improve.

Gaiety is joyfulness, lightheartedness, and the jollification of life's moments. We find opportunities to be joyful, and liberate ourselves to feel and show our delight.

- Instead of scolding a student for an outburst, we may offer a good-natured quip instead.
- We may help a colleague see the humor in an event that she found disturbing.
- As we walk in the door of our school, we treat those hallowed halls as possibilities for experiencing joy and delight.

These three G's brace us for what needs to be done, drive us to complete our task, and spur us to be exultant about achievements large and small. They bolster us to teach with vitality!

86 | WHEN WE ARE WHAT WE DO

For some of us, teaching becomes a habit. Not only do we take our work (teaching) home with us, we also take it to banks, to restaurants, and on public transportation. We believe we are doing a valuable service by correcting others, suggesting alternative ways of doing something, and explaining an idea past the point of the listener's interest. Some educators seem proud to announce that they are workaholics, that they never stop teaching. But is that a *good* thing?

Buying a ticket for a movie, we take the opportunity to discuss the meaning of an unusual movie title with the young employee. A neighbor's car won't start, and we expound on the mechanical functions that could be at fault. A child is running around a restaurant nearly colliding with others, and we lean forward, in front of her parents, and suggest that she sit down at her table.

Being a teacher prepares us for so many things in life. And vigorously aspiring to be our best is one of the habits of mind that we embrace. Yet it is worth asking if our "teacher self" is consuming us . . . *and* consuming our families and friends. Variety in interests and activities provides a reservoir and a respite from school life. These kinds of "vacations from teaching" do not diminish our vitality; they sustain it.

Our families beg for our attention; we have no acquaintances beyond those at school; we have no interests other than our school work; we cannot silence our thoughts about school long enough to have interludes of other activities and interests; we assume others are as interested in our "school stories" as we are; we have no borders that separate our work from our non-school lives. When thoughts of school consume us, we may be exemplifying the idea that "We are what we do." Our identities and activities may not have developed beyond our "teaching self."

"Teaching is my life" is poetic. But, strictly interpreted, it is not necessarily healthy. What if spending time outside the arena of schoolwork and school relationships is one of the best ways to preserve or regain our vitality *for* school, our vitality for teaching?

Our total commitment to our students and our teaching is admirable and noble. Yet the concerning word is "total." When we offer ourselves a buffer between what we do and who we are, we pave the pathway toward a balanced, fruitful, and satisfying life.

Someone once asked: "When we are what we do, then who are we when we don't?" Hmmmmm . . .

87 | INTERPRETING BEHAVIOR

How we interpret behaviors determines the ways we respond to them. For the benefit of ourselves, our students, and our co-workers, it can be helpful to rethink the ways we see common behaviors. A three-phase process can structure our interpretations.

1. *Observe.* Pause to broaden your view. Is the student intentionally breaking the rules, misbehaving, harming? Or is the student oblivious, distracted? What do you see?
2. *Interpret.* Ask, "What else *could* it be?" Pause to consider innocent motives. The shift from home to school behaviors can be drastic and difficult for some. What do you think?
3. *Respond.* Feel inner calm as you firmly address the student and the behavior. Response can be a simply stated command without criticism, judgment, or punishment. Escalating consequences occur as necessary. How do you act?

Sometimes, especially in tough situations, we can become pouncers who "run a tight ship" and pride ourselves on how fast we exert control. So what differences might behavior reinterpretation make?

Loud talking may be forgetting to speak quietly. Bumping into another may be the usual way friends play. Profanity or lewd gestures may be normal behaviors at home. Outbursts of shoving, laughing, joking, and insulting may reflect how students live during the many hours they are not in school.

Neutral directives, with varying degrees of firmness, can deliver the desired expectation without accusation or excessive scolding.

- "The noise level is way too high right now. Fix it."
- "Toby, you are interrupting Jamey. Listen."
- "If your voice is too loud, I'm going to assume you are not listening."
- "Physical roughness doesn't belong in this school."
- "Language like that is not acceptable here."

When we momentarily reserve judgment about students' behaviors, we may be more likely to acknowledge that, outside our classrooms and schools, the behaviors we find offensive may be acceptable and preferable. Once we interpret the possible motives of students' behaviors, we are direct about what needs to change without demeaning the student or the behavior.

88 | ON SECOND THOUGHT

In 1960s America, a popular motto was "If it feels good, do it." The message was intended to lift societal constraints on beliefs and behaviors. But for some, the motto's sentiment spiked widespread encouragement to reject inhibitions, to be free of restraint. "Do whatever you want, whenever you want, however you want" was the message. "Inhibition" became a dirty word.

Yet inhibitions are critically important to maturity and societal conventions. The ability to inhibit appropriately and delay gratification (even if momentarily) signals development.

The phrase "on second thought" offers a strategy for taking a moment to think about our thinking, to metacognate about our decisions: "What else could it be?" "What else could I choose?" "What are my options?" We take a moment to allow our better selves to make better decisions:

- Stifling laughter, delaying an opinion, suspending the impulse to offer assistance
- Modifying a reply, choosing a kinder adjective, opting for silence

- Resisting a second helping, choosing a healthy alternative, deciding to pass on a risky behavior

Not the same as second-guessing, second thoughts prepare us to be deliberate rather than impulsive, reflective rather than pejorative, strategic rather than reactionary.

Some teachers may innately use second thoughts in school relationships and teaching. But, others of us may not have considered this notion as a strategy. With the possibility of allowing us to reframe, revise, and revive our interactions with others, why not experiment with second thoughts? On second thought, why not declare a "Second Thoughts Day?"

89 | COMPASSION FATIGUE

Is it possible to care too much? Teachers care. We want the best for our students and colleagues and communities. Yet some of us may *care too much* about others' feelings, personal struggles, and life challenges.

When we absorb all the bad news, our lenses get foggy. We worry beyond the bounds of our abilities to help. We begin to believe that fixing the problem is futile, that we cannot make a difference in such a quagmire. We give our *selves* away. The helpers become the victims. Caregivers become needy of care.

When compassion fatigue overwhelms, we must develop strategies for self-care. Maintaining strength to help others is necessary, even when that strength must include a professional distance, a sense of separateness. *Self-compassion is necessary to maintain stamina and avoid compassion fatigue in schools.*

Cultivating a rich personal life may include pursuing personal, social, physical, and spiritual activities that calm us, inform us, and give us sustenance. We learn to care for ourselves in ways that matter.

90 | CATASTROPHIZING

Does your imagination ever leap from a simple thought to a dramatic conclusion? Do you habitually think, "Something bad is going to result from this"? If these are typical habits of thought for you, you may be a catastrophizer.

Those of us who are expert catastrophizers may cause our friends and family to become minimizers in order to counterbalance our overstatements. They see us as always thinking the worst, seeing only the dark side, and being overly suspicious. Do we want to live our lives imagining the next catastrophe?

A humorous example of catastrophic thinking occurred when a graduate student walked into class, his feet shuffling and his shoulders slumping. "What's wrong?" asked the professor.

"My paper is late. I didn't get it finished," replied the student.

The student seemed to be taking one tardy paper as a sign of failure. So the professor decided to play along. "So, you are submitting a late paper . . . which means you'll get a bad grade . . . which means you'll flunk the course . . . which means you won't get your degree . . . which means you won't get a job . . . which means you have to give up your apartment . . . which means you'll be living under a bridge."

All laughed as the student looked up with a wry grin and said, "You've been reading my diary."

When we envision a spiral of catastrophe, the dramatic consequences can be excessive, especially *within* us. Our bodies can react with jolts of adrenaline, and we feel the tension as if the worst has already happened. Our bodies and minds may suffer as if the catastrophe is real.

- A parent who made an unkind remark to us five years ago is elected to the school board. We begin imagining her influence on our future at the school.
- Testing is three days away, and several students have been absent for test preparation sessions. We cannot stop worrying about how poorly these students may score on the tests, and how the test results may affect our already rocky relationship with the principal.
- Rumors persist about a possible school strike, loss of programs, and teacher layoffs. We become hypervigilant, watching for clues about our future. We lose sleep while ruminating about the financial prospects for our family. And we fall deeper and deeper into the ennui of our imagination.

For your own good health, stop the runaway imaginings. End the catastrophizing. Believe in your resilience. Instead of believing the worst, take back your strength, reject the helplessness, and affirm, "I wouldn't let that happen."

91 | MOMENTS OF GRACE

"What a nasty thing to say!" But was it?

"Her tantrums are so immature!" But are they?

"He is just lazy and doesn't care." But is he?

A momentary pause between our observation and our conclusion about someone can make a world of difference. That moment of grace, in some ways, bestows a peace offering on someone who may or may not deserve it. It offers vitality and goodwill to the encounter.

During that momentary internal pause, we have the opportunity to broaden our interpretation, to look beyond our immediate response, to offer the benefit of the doubt. The "nasty thing to say" may be a misunderstood remark. Those "immature tantrums" may be the result of severe emotional pain. That "laziness" may be depression or disillusionment.

Few of us would argue with someone giving *us* the benefit of the doubt. Most often we would welcome that generosity. Yet how do we offer a moment of grace without being gullible?

When our intent is to suspend judgment momentarily, we are neither believing nor disbelieving. We simply postpone our conclusions about another's meaning and intention because we do not know the full story, and we *know* that we don't know. We are comfortable sitting with our gesture of grace.

Even though we may be taking this high road for the other, the benefits of grace ripple to us as well. Silent moments of grace serve both the giver and the receiver. Opportunities for grace are everywhere.

> A moment of grace is the interval of time we take to reframe somebody's behavior so that we can react with curiosity, compassion, or openness rather than judgment, annoyance, or defensiveness. Giving someone the benefit of doubt allows us to delay our reaction to the comment or action with the intent of looking beyond our immediate response. (Bennett & Bartholomew, 1997, p. 210)

92 | POSITIONAL AND PERSONAL POWER

Positional power surrounds us. Parents, supervisors, elected officials, siblings, reporters . . . they all have power to make choices for us, and sometimes about us. Yet it is our *personal* power that provides our quality of life.

Personal power is knowing our strength and using it to balance and rebalance our thoughts and behaviors. We know we will fail. We know we will become entangled in difficult situations. We know we will lose sight of our best selves at times. Yet our power is sustained by the belief that we will regain our footing. We will overcome our challenges. We will persevere and regain our ultimate vibrancy.

Those with personal power display their confidence and competence, but not at another's expense. They know their strength and use it to continually strive for interpersonal satisfaction, connection, and meaning.

What makes our personal power strong? It is the influence generated and exuded. This version of personal power is not necessarily influence *over* others; rather, it inspires others in ways that make them want to be better, do better. Think of the people you have met, perhaps even strangers who appear powerful. They seem comfortable in their own skin, awake to all that is around them.

Our personal power is "our spiritual fingerprint" (Rusk, 1993, p. 47). It is magnificent in its subtlety and stability. When we acknowledge and use our personal power to its best intention, we see and feel its influence on us.

Positional power ranks us according to our positions in the social, familial, administrative, or business-related milieu of our lives. The influence of positional power can vary greatly, and the extent to which people submit to positional power varies greatly. We forfeit an important part of ourselves when we sublimate personal power in favor of our own or another's positional power (Rusk, 1993, p. 46).

Have you noticed that some of the most influential teachers in schools may be those who are powerfully quiet and unassuming? Have you noticed that students can sometimes sense the power of a classmate who otherwise is not an obvious leader?

As we ponder the distinctions and possibilities of these different powers, it is important to consider a relationship between the two. When personal power thrives, positional power almost becomes irrelevant. (Rusk, 1993, p. 47)

93 | LOOK FOR THE CHARM

Sometimes we become so focused on the turmoil, we forget to see the charm that surrounds us. Consumed by our to-do lists and home obligations, we forget to look, listen, and feel.

Plenty of obstacles can devitalize teachers. And sometimes we can get in the habit of stewing in our malaise. So we must be intentional about looking for and absorbing the charming sights, sounds, and feelings that surround us. Like vitamins for the soul, moments of charm can boost and revive.

The simplest things can bring us back to the roots and bounty of our lives: The giggle of a child. The good-natured sparring of teenagers. The fearlessly perched raven watching traffic from a stop sign. The pattern of a spiderweb and the brilliance of the spider that wove it. The easy laughter of friends. The look of wonder when a student "gets it." The beauty of young musicians as they personify music. The brisk gait of an elderly neighbor. The pure joy of singing with abandon. The first sip of your morning coffee. The scent of a book. The frenzied cheers of parents at a sporting event. The embracing hug of a loved one. The luxury of living without pain. The buzz of energy when school begins and ends.

The allure of these charming moments can be smothered by our intense focus on work and troubles. Yes, these simple moments of charm are always there for us . . . when we notice them. We can inhale their whimsy and encourage ourselves to smile, laugh, and be glad for the moment.

Seeing, hearing, and appreciating simple things returns the aesthetic to our anesthetic worlds. When we look for and *feel* those moments of charm, we can be grateful. Those moments remind us we are alive in the world.

94 | CIVILITY

Sometimes we live as if we have two categories of feelings toward others: we like them or we dislike them. If we adopt this stance, we are missing out on so much we could learn.

"Liking" may be the least substantial opinion we can have. Liking is highly overrated. Civility, however, is not.

Politeness, courtesy, respect, graciousness, consideration—those are just some of the synonyms and images of civility.

As we imagine those with whom we come in contact in our neighborhoods, cities, organizations, and businesses, there is likely a wide array of affinity. Yet camaraderie need not determine the level of civility we display.

When we present attitudes and behaviors of civility, both in and out of school, we reap the benefits of knowing we are doing our best. We are behaving respectfully.

Civility . . . is the set of sacrifices we make for the sake of our common journey with others, and out of love and respect for the very idea that there *are* others. When we are civil, we are not pretending to like those we actually despise; we are not pretending to hold any attitude toward them except that we accept and value them as every bit our equals . . . . The duty to love our neighbors . . . is not lessened because we happen to think our neighbor is wrong about a few things. (Carter, 1998, p. 23)

95 | BOUNCE

Have you noticed that every day, every hour, there is opportunity to bounce? It might be a funny expression from your dog, a clever image on a T-shirt, a surprising comment by a student, an endearing story from a colleague, or the sweet expression of a parent's love.

Each of these moments, and so many more, are provided for us *all the time*. They surround us. When we know to look for them, when we are open enough to notice them, we can feel the bounce that energizes us, at *least* momentarily.

Our worries and tensions can absorb us in our days at school. That takes no effort. But allowing ourselves to be saturated with that heaviness is also allowing ourselves to be captives of our troubling thoughts and harried schedules.

We can take a moment to shrug it off. Loosen the crust of tension and protection. Open ourselves to spotting and feeling moments that bounce.

Teachers can adopt the habit of looking for and feeling the bounce in our lives. And when we do, we give ourselves a dose of vigor. We revive.

When we give access to the appealing and delightful possibilities that rehumanize us, we change ourselves. We smile. We love. We connect to beauty. We become resilient. We feel the bounce.

96 | PARANOIA PANDEMIC

Like a sickness, paranoia can destroy goodwill and relationships in schools. It takes so little, at times, to ferment suspicion of intentional ill will.

Once we begin to suspect something is amiss, we look for confirmation. We look for evidence that someone is doing harm to our reputation or sabotaging our relationships. We experience one betrayal or infraction, and we can't let go of viewing someone through that lens. Surprisingly, when we look so hard for evidence of harm, we can usually find it, even when it *does not exist*.

- Certain members of your teaching team begin gathering for happy hour, but not all are invited. You begin suspecting that they plan to propose sweeping changes to the department.
- Your tenure is pending. When a teacher who serves on the tenure committee sighs, "It's been a rough day" as he leaves the meeting, you begin worrying that trouble is lurking for your future at the school.
- You notice a teacher and a student standing alone in the hallway, and as you approach, they both stop talking and look

embarrassed and uncomfortable. You wonder if their suspicious behavior hints at an unethical relationship.

At times of high-stakes turmoil, paranoia can become pandemic in schools. It is up to individuals to guard against it. What do we do when paranoia lurks?

- Use "second thoughts" to disprove your opinion.
- Dismantle the thinking that can blind you to innocent or less sensational interpretations.
- Calmly and confidently ask the person you have concerns about if there is a problem, or if you are misinterpreting some behaviors or actions.
- Strengthen yourself by knowing that you can make amends for any misunderstandings.
- Reconnect with your honor and good intentions.

Renewed affirmations of vitality are the benefits of these actions. We *feel* our powerful spirit return to us, and our aliveness signals our revived personal strength.

97 | BE IMPECCABLE WITH YOUR WORD

"Faultless," "flawless," "unimpeachable," "without harm": these words define impeccability.

Being impeccable with our words means that we are closely attentive to their meanings, their power, and their lasting effects. Are we vigilant about the words we use to instruct and converse? Are we careful to speak accurately and thoughtfully during meetings and informal encounters?

In *The Four Agreements,* Ruiz describes our word as a force, "not just a sound or a written symbol" (1997, p. 26). Words are powerful because they reflect and communicate our thoughts. That is why we need to aspire to speak without harm: words show who we are.

Like a sword with two edges, our words can build or destroy, sting or fawn. Are we aware of what our words are doing? Do we speak "without harm" to ourselves? Our inner self-talk is nearly constant. What we say to *ourselves* can be every bit as powerful as what we say to *others*.

Sometimes exaggeration becomes a habit, but it is not necessarily a harmless one. Exaggeration rarely serves us well, and it can erode our believability. When we habitually speak in extremes or we inflate our experiences, we serve no one, including ourselves. It can be nearly impossible for someone to unhear what she heard. And once trust and credibility are pierced, it can be nearly impossible to regain them. School communities, with their many invested constituents, deserve careful, impeccable use of words.

Consider the influence of the words in the contrasting pairs that follow. These "I" statements show the subtle differences in how we describe ourselves. If you say them aloud, notice the reaction of your body to the words.

- "I am exhausted"; "I am fatigued."
- "I am scared"; "I am uneasy."
- "I am stupid"; "I am confused."
- "I am nervous"; "I am excited."
- "I am stressed"; "I feel the pressure."
- "She shouted at me"; "She raised her voice."
- "It was the worst day of my life"; "It wasn't my best day."

Experiment. See what happens when your words are impeccable, accurate, and kind.

> Be impeccable with your word. Speak with integrity. Say only what you mean. Avoid using the word to speak against yourself or to gossip about others. Use the power of your word in the direction of truth and love. (Ruiz, 1997)

98 | DON'T MAKE ASSUMPTIONS

Ruiz advises, "Don't make assumptions." Assuming we know another's meaning and motive is as unreliable as them knowing ours.

- We are not selected for a leadership position we wanted. We translate this as "I'm not as strong a leader as he is."
- We learn of a parent complaint about us. We refute, "She's a habitual complainer and has no idea what she's talking about."
- We are greeted warmly and happily by a colleague who is usually less dramatic. We assume, "She must want something from me."

If we would take one day to monitor our assumptions, it may be eye-opening, even life-opening. Making an assumption is not the same as drawing a conclusion. Conclusions are reasoned suppositions. Assumptions are often automatic and habitual. We may not know we have them, so we don't challenge them. We may also be aghast at the assumptions others make about us.

A "No Assumptions Day" can change the style and content of our communications. It can challenge us to be clear with others about our own intentions and reasons. Shedding assumptions can liberate. It can illuminate. It can revitalize.

Don't make assumptions. Find the courage to ask questions and to express what you really want. Communicate with others as clearly as you can to avoid misunderstandings, sadness, and drama. With just this one agreement, you can completely transform your life. (Ruiz, 1997)

99 | DON'T TAKE ANYTHING PERSONALLY

Whatever anyone else says and does, it is about them. Whatever you say and do, it is about you. So writes Ruiz in *The Four Agreements*.

When someone begins a conversation with "Now don't take this personally," many of us want to run and hide. We sense that what is coming will not be pleasant to hear.

"Don't take this personally" is often a prelude to criticizing: "That was really awful." The phrase seems to give the speaker permission to say hurtful things. Would we ever say, "Don't take this personally, but I think you're a really great teacher"? Doubtful.

Ruiz writes, however, that neither the compliments we welcome nor the complaints that make us bristle are about us. Only what *we* say is about us. That's all. Of the four agreements Ruiz describes, this one seems to surprise and challenge us most. Yet it also may be the most liberating, once we understand and absorb it.

Not taking anything personally unbinds us from the thoughts and opinions of the speaker.

- When we do not take anything personally, we free ourselves to let others "say what they say" without affecting us.
- We do not take others' opinions as our own. We simply listen curiously.
- We are less consumed by others' words and deeds. We feel a buffer of separation.
- We watch, listen, and sometimes wonder what caused a particular reaction.
- We look at and examine another's compliment or complaint as if it were her new sweater. It has nothing to do with us.

"Nothing others say and do is because of us" also means that nothing we say and do is because of *them*. Well, that may be a bit unsettling, right?

If I tell you that you are a troublemaker or that you are beautiful, wouldn't that be about *you*? Nope. My compliments and criticisms are about *me* and *my* thoughts, my conclusions.

Accepting this idea may take a while. You may well feel like arguing about this. Why not try it on for a few days and see what happens with your students, colleagues, administrators, and staff?

Reorienting our thoughts so that we can experience the resulting freedom can be both rewarding and liberating. Taking nothing personally can revitalize us in schools and homes, because we learn not to be consumed and subsumed by others' words and actions.

> Nothing others do is because of you. What others say and do is a projection of their own reality . . . . When you are immune to the opinions and actions of others, you won't be the victim of needless suffering. (Ruiz, 1997)

100 | ALWAYS DO YOUR BEST

"Always do your best" is the agreement that Ruiz believes will most help the other three agreements (1997, p. 75). Being our best is about intention. When we intend to do our best, we are relieved from always thinking we should be more and do more.

Are there times when we do less than our best? More than our best? Do we know what our best is? Do we even pay attention to such things?

Doing less than our best keeps us from feeling satisfied, secure, and fulfilled. We are less vigorous, less vivacious. There can be a domino effect leading from feeling disappointed to feeling hopeless to "I give up. I'm just not good at this."

Some of us may specialize in less than our best. We wing it or make do instead of planning substantial lessons and creating thorough reports. We avoid helping even when we are available. We gossip about students or co-workers. We silently compete with others on the staff. All of us can likely recognize ourselves in each of these moments. It is normal to be "less than our best" at times.

Some of us may specialize in doing more than our best. We make commitments that we cannot keep, because we are determined to keep ourselves active. We refuse to take a break, even though we would benefit from fresh air and a change of pace. We know our reputation relies on student achievements, so we invest too heavily in making students appear successful.

By now, it may be obvious that our "best" changes. Various factors influence what our best can be on any given day, in any given setting.

Sometimes doing " better" is a reasonable and worthy target: it's good enough. Adopting the intent to do our best means we can know and accept that whatever our best is in this moment, it's good enough for now. We can say: "That's as good as I can do right now." "This will do for today." "Maybe tomorrow I'll be able to do a better job at that." Imagine how our students could benefit from such reasonable self-acceptance about "doing our best."

> Your best is going to change from moment to moment; it will be different when you are healthy as opposed to sick. Under any circumstance, simply do your best, and you will avoid self-judgment, self-abuse, and regret. (Ruiz, 1997)

101 | PEACEFUL, POWERFUL YOU!

"You can't change what you don't acknowledge," as Dr. Phil McGraw said. "When we know better, we do better," said Maya Angelou. Tenets such as these remind us that *knowing* paves a path toward personal power. That *doing* furnishes opportunities for personal peacefulness.

Tempers rise. Feelings hurt. Resilience flees. When these things happen in schools, it's time to inhale, stand tall, and get to work . . . on ourselves! This book has reminded us that there are *peaceful* ways to intervene. It has also informed us that there is *power* in our choice of words and behaviors. With the balance of peace and power, we can help mend the turmoil.

We need not give up personal peace for power or personal power for peace. Peace and power reside in our ability to be generous of spirit, to recast meanings, and to minimize fear. We see others' troubles as their own, even as we care about them. We problem-solve ways to alleviate difficulties, even as we know the quest is likely infinite and "letting go" can be a wise choice.

Teaching with Vitality reminds us that we are powerful in shaping our lives and the quality of our relationships. We recognize our always-growing, always-changing internal resources for reconnecting with students, co-workers, and parents. If we don't know what to do, we search for ways to understand and act. We resolve to do better, one step at a time.

You now have many options for considering your course. You have many perspectives from which to make your choices.

Though it may *appear* that we are working to fix *others'* behaviors, *we* are the beneficiaries: we change our minds to change our perspectives, to change our relationships, to change ourselves. And through it all, we can revive. We can thrive. We can find ourselves on the path to health and wellness in our schools and in our communities. And, we can see vitality return to our teaching.

REFERENCES

Batchelor, S. (2004, December). Can you see others as they see themselves? O, the Oprah Magazine

Bennett, P. D. (1988). The perils and profits of praise. Music Educators Journal, 75(1), 22–24.

Bennett, P. D. (1999). Metaphorically teaching: The use of imagery in preparing teachers. The Mountain Lake Reader, 1, 50–54.

Bennett, P. D. (2010, November). The power of brevity: Two word cues. MEI News and Notes.

Bennett, P. D. (2012, January). Valuing the volley: What dogs and tennis can teach us about teaching and living. MEI News and Notes.

Bennett, P. D. (2016). Questioning the unmusical ways we teach children music. In C. Abril & B. Gault (Eds.), Teaching general music: Approaches, issues, and viewpoints (pp. 286–307). New York: Oxford University Press.

Bennett, P., & Bartholomew, D. R. (1997). SongWorks 1: Singing in the education of children. Van Nuys, CA: Wadsworth.

Bennett, P. D., & Suarez, V. (2016, August). Vitality: Reviving the life in your teaching. Southwestern Musician, 12–14.

Bowling, D., & Hoffman, D. (2003). Bringing peace into the room. San Francisco: Jossey-Bass.

Brown, S. (2009). Play is more than fun. TED Talk, March 12. Available on YouTube: https://youtu.be/HHwXlcHcTHc.

Bush, R. A. B., & Folger, J. P. (1994). The promise of mediation: Responding to conflict through empowerment and recognition. San Francisco: Jossey-Bass.

Cain, S. (2012). *Quiet: The power of introverts in a world that can't stop talking.* New York: Crown.

Carroll, M. (2006). *Awake at work: 35 practical Buddhist principles for discovering clarity and balance in the midst of work's chaos.* Boston: Shambhala.

Carter, S. (1998). *Civility: Manners, morals, and the etiquette of democracy.* New York: HarperPerennial.

Charles, C. M. (1985). *Building classroom discipline: From models to practice.* New York: Longman.

Cooper, M. (1984). *Change your voice, change your life.* New York: Macmillan.

Curwin, R. L., & Mendler, A. N. (1997). *As tough as necessary: Countering violence, aggression, and hostility in our schools.* Alexandria, VA: Association for Supervision and Curriculum Development.

Dalai Lama, & Cutler, H. (1998). *The art of happiness: A handbook for living.* New York: Riverhead Books.

De Angelis, B. (1994). *Real moments.* New York: Delacorte Press.

Fuller, Robert. (2003). *Somebodies and nobodies: Overcoming the abuse of rank.* Gabriola Island, BC: New Society Publishers.

Hart, L. A. (1983). *Human brain and human learning.* New York: Longman.

Hifler, J. S. (1992). *A Cherokee feast of days.* Tulsa, OK: Council Oaks Books.

Jacks, L. P. (1932). *Education and recreation.* New York: Harper and Brothers.

Jones, F. H. (1987). *Positive classroom discipline.* New York: McGraw-Hill.

Kohn, A. (1992). *No contest: The case against competition.* Rev. ed. New York: Houghton Mifflin.

Kohn, A. (1993). *Punished by rewards: The trouble with gold stars, incentive plans, A's, and other bribes.* Rev. ed. Boston: Houghton Mifflin.

McGinnis, A. L. (1985). *Bringing out the best in people: How to enjoy helping others excel.* Minneapolis, MN: Augsburg Publishing House.

Noddings, N. (2003). *Happiness and education.* Cambridge, UK: Cambridge University Press.

Raessler, K. R. (2003). *Aspiring to excel: Leadership initiatives for music educators.* Chicago: GIA.

Rama, S., Ballentine, R., & Hymes, A. (1979). *The science of breath: A practical guide.* Honesdale, PA: Himalayan International Institute of Yoga Science and Philosophy.

Ruiz, D. M. (1997). *The four agreements: A practical guide to personal freedom.* San Rafael, CA: Amber-Allen.

Rusk, T. (1993). *The power of ethical persuasion: Winning through understanding at work and at home.* New York: Penguin.

Sutton Smith, B. (1998). *The Ambiguity of Play.* Cambridge, MA: Harvard University Press.

Ury, W. (1993). *Getting past no: Negotiating your way from confrontation to cooperation.* New York: Bantam.